S H A R K

S H A R K

Endangered Predator of the Sea

Marty Snyderman

Photography by Marty Snyderman

KEY PORTER BOOKS

The publisher gratefully acknowledges the assistance of the Canada Council, the Ontario Publishing Centre and the Ontario Arts Council.

Canadian Cataloguing and Publication Data

Snyderman, Marty
Shark: endangered predator of the sea

Includes index.
ISBN 1-55013-629-1 (pb)
ISBN 1-55013-781-6 (hc)

1. Sharks. 2. Wildlife conservation 3. Nature photography. I. Title.

QL638.9.S58 1995   597'.31   C95-931367-2

PAGE 1: BLUE SHARKS ARE RELATIVELY COMMON AND ARE OFTEN SEEN IN MOVIES AND DOCUMENTARY FILMS.

PAGES 2 AND 3: A GRAY REEF SHARK CRUISES OVER A SEA FAN IN THE CORAL SEA.

PAGE 4: A BLUE SHARK CRUISES AT THE SURFACE BELOW ITS OWN REFLECTION IN THE OPEN SEA.

PAGE 5: THE UNUSUAL SHAPE OF THE HEAD OF THE HAMMERHEAD SHARK PROVIDES LIFT LIKE THE WING OF AN AIRPLANE AT THE FRONT END OF THE BODY.

PAGE 7: LIKE WHALE SHARKS, BASKING SHARKS, AND SEVERAL OTHER SPECIES, MANTA RAYS ARE FILTER FEEDERS, CONSUMING LARGE QUANTITIES OF PLANKTON.

PAGE 8: AS A FORM OF CAMOUFLAGE, GREAT WHITES ARE DISTINCTLY COUNTERSHADED, BEING DARKLY HUED ON THE TOP AND LIGHTLY COLORED ON THE UNDERBELLY.

Key Porter Books Limited
70 The Esplanade
Toronto, Ontario
M5E 1R2

Design: Annabelle Stanley
Printed and bound in Hong Kong
96 97 98 99 6 5 4 3 2 1

THE PUBLISHERS WISH TO ACKNOWLEDGE THE HELP OF DR. CHRIS HARVEY-CLARK, DIRECTOR OF ANIMAL CARE, DALHOUSIE UNIVERSITY, HALIFAX, NOVA SCOTIA.

CONTENTS

ACKNOWLEDGMENTS

Over the years I have dived with many people who know a lot about sharks. There is simply no way I would have been in a position either to be asked to write this book, or to have taken so many pictures of sharks, or even to have had so much fun, without their help. It only seems right that I take a minute to thank my pals. Thanks to Howard and Michele Hall, Bob and Cathy Cranston, Carl Roessler and the gang at See & Sea Travel, John and Noreen McKenney, Mark Conlin, Norbert Wu, Dan Walsh, Mike Brock, Ron Hyatt, Tom Allen, Stuart Cove, Madison Quartiano, Georgette Belcher, Maryan Smith, Rodney Fox, Fred Fisher, Mike deGruy, G.G. Waggoner Jr., Joe and Chester Storthz, and Ron and Valerie Taylor. Let's do it some more!

SHARK!

SHARK! THE WORD ALONE CONJURES UP sheer horror in the minds of many. Indeed, few images from nature are as powerful and dramatic as that of a large, cold-eyed shark, mouth agape and razor-edged teeth fully exposed, swimming right for you. Blood-thirsty, ruthless killers, ready and able to eat anything that crosses their path, including their own kind – so sharks have been portrayed in recent years, at least in the Western world.

In the religion, mythology, and lore of some non-Western societies, sharks are viewed in an entirely different light. Throughout the South Pacific, islanders have long viewed sharks in various roles, ranging from vengeful god to guardian spirit. In the ancient ceremonies of some of these island nations, human sacrifices to shark deities were not uncommon.

LEFT: FOUND IN TROPICAL AND SEMITROPICAL SEAS AROUND THE WORLD, WHALE SHARKS ARE THE WORLD'S LARGEST FISH, REACHING LENGTHS IN EXCESS OF 40 FEET (12 M) AND WEIGHING 30,000 TO 50,000 POUNDS (13,600 TO 22,680 KG) WHEN FULLY GROWN. ALTHOUGH THEY HAVE A DOCILE NATURE, THEIR SHEER SIZE CAUSES FEAR.

In the Solomon Islands sharks are deified and are said to live in sacred caverns, complete with stone altars, in coastal lagoons. In Vietnam, the whale shark, Ca Ong, was thought to stand watch over the people and protect the shoreline. Stone temples honoring the mighty creature still dot the coast, next to abandoned gunneries and tanks.

In Hawaii, sharks are still seen as reincarnated ancestors, and killing one is a forbidden act. Native Hawaiians believed that Kama-Hoa-Lii, the king of the sharks, lived in the waters of Honolulu harbor, while the shark queen, Oahu, resided on the sea floor in the same area. Ancient sea legends tell of a beautiful girl named Kalei, whom Kama-Hoa-Lii fell in love with when he saw her swimming. With the magical powers accorded a king, he turned himself into a man, and together they had a son named Nanaue. On his back, Nanaue bore a birthmark that resembled a shark's mouth. The king decreed that Nanaue was never to be given meat, but that commandment was violated; the taste of meat led Nanaue to the discovery that he could turn himself into a shark. As his craving for more and more meat took hold, he cruised the waters in his new form, attacking islanders to satisfy his hunger, until he was caught and buried on the plot of land currently known as Shark Hill.

For many centuries, neighboring Tongans revered sharks as guardian spirits, and to this day commercial divers there seek them out. By contrast, in Polynesian lore, the shark deity, Kauhuhu, lived inside a great undersea cavern, preying on all who entered, and natives of New Guinea regarded sharks as evil and dangerous wizards, making it taboo to catch one.

In other parts of the world, as far away as Africa and the Pacific Northwest, ancient societies recognized a special quality in sharks. A variety of African tribes considered shark spirits to possess special powers for warding off and overcoming danger. Worshipped dutifully, these spirits were capable of offering protection; however, when not paid proper respect, the spirits of the sharks inflicted evil and misfortune. Some African tribal art still features the shark mask. In the decorative art of the Indians of the Pacific Northwest, images of the dogfish shark featured prominently, serving as a reminder of a woman who was taken away by a shark and then became one.

Chinese seamen long believed that sharks could sense when someone aboard ship was dying and would follow the ship until the body was finally cast into the sea. In the nineteenth century, the families of many Chinese immigrants who eventually settled in California spent considerable sums of money having the remains of deceased family members transported to China by ship so they could be buried with their ancestors. The seamen who manned these vessels commonly swore that the sharks knew what was aboard and followed the ships for days on end.

In the West, we seem to view the beliefs and perceptions of what we consider to be primitive cultures as interesting, and sometimes amusing, but our view of the shark is no less primal and superstitious. Sailors from European nations often pinned the tail of a shark to the bowsprit for good luck. King Edward II, the ruler of England from 1307 to 1327, proclaimed the sturgeon a royal fish; all sturgeon caught belonged to the king. This practice in England was not much different from that in the Pacific Islands, where sharks were accorded a similar distinction: in some South Pacific cultures, any fisherman who could catch a shark and bring it to his king was given special status.

The origin of the English word "shark" is linked to our long-standing perception of these often misrepresented creatures. The etymological roots can be traced back to the German word "shurke," meaning villain, and to the Anglo-Saxon "sceron," meaning cutting or shearing. Ever since Elizabethan times, the word "shark" has been used evocatively to suggest certain characteristics. Consider the phrases "loan shark," "card shark," and "pool shark." Similarly, almost everyone understands the punch line of the joke "Why won't a shark bite a lawyer? Professional courtesy." The point is that the Western world, too, casts some creatures in a certain light, and that portrayal colors the way we use and value them. Our perception of sharks has been molded by the way they are portrayed on television, in Hollywood films, and in our literature.

For the past five years, the Discovery Channel has broadcast a series titled *Shark Week*. In terms of the numbers of viewers who tune in, the series has been a smash hit. While there is a lot of good information in the programs that air during *Shark Week*, the slant is generally toward meeting viewers' expectations: clearly film sequences showing big blue sharks gnawing on divers wearing chain-mail suits and great white sharks ripping into bait get more air time than do scenes of horn sharks resting on a rocky reef at the bottom of a kelp forest.

While television series like *Flipper* cast dolphins in a warm light, films like *The Deep*, *Sharks' Treasure*, and *Jaws* and its sequels capitalized on and further exploited the Western view of sharks as vicious, man-eating monsters. While we like to think of ourselves as being too sophisticated to buy in to such portrayals, our perceptions of sharks as evil, marauding eating machines are deeply rooted in Western literature.

As far back as A.D. 79, Pliny the Elder, in his noted *Historia Naturalis*, mentioned the shark. Even Shakespeare had his say: in Act 4, scene 1, of *Macbeth*, he made "maw and gulf / Of the ravin'd, salt-sea shark" an ingredient for the Witches' caldron.

Hemingway wrote admiringly of the power and fight of the mako shark in *The Old Man and the Sea*. Other works such as Horace Mazet's *Shark! Shark!* glorified the feats of those who hunt sharks. Author Zane Grey penned a number of highly publicized accounts of his exploits and battles with sharks while big-game fishing in the Pacific.

However, no work featuring sharks has had anywhere near the impact of *Jaws*, by Peter Benchley, a book that indelibly imprinted the great white shark on the cultures of America, Europe, Australia, and other segments of the globe. The great white shark has since become a symbol, representing the world's more than 350 species of shark.

What beach-goers haven't heard the throbbing-heartbeat, da-dum, da-dum, da-dum of the theme song to the film playing in their heads during an uneasy moment? Of course, in Hollywood's versions of *Jaws*, the sharks grew to fanciful sizes and were driven to unnatural feats as far-fetched as threatening a helicopter. Somehow, these excesses have been unfairly attributed to Benchley, and some members of the sport-diving community have vilified him for frightening away potential customers, while some naturalists have condemned him for glorifying and supposedly popularizing the wholesale killing of sharks. The truth is that Peter, a friend with whom I have worked on several occasions over the years, did his research and attests to the fact that everything that the great white in his book did or was said to have done can be attributed to some great white shark somewhere. The hyperbole is Hollywood's, not Benchley's. In an enlightening comment offered in his own defense, he once told me: "I write for a reasonably educated reader. Some people choose to be ignorant, and I can't change that. What I try to do is educate and entertain those who allow themselves to be educated and entertained. I love the sea and the great white shark. That is why I had the passion to write this story."

Studies conducted by renowned psychotherapist Jon Magnuson provide a fascinating insight into the way Western cultures perceive sharks and highlight the "contrast between expectation and fact, between image and data." As Magnuson points out, humans' intense fear of sharks is groundless. The International Shark Attack File, a study that documents shark attacks worldwide, has recorded 1,500 attacks on humans since the year 1560. While recent statistics suggest the number of shark attacks might be as high as 50 to 100 annually, far more people die from everyday kinds of accidents, a fact that receives very little public attention.

Magnuson attributes the disparity between the facts and the fear to the way sharks are "projected," a psychological term that refers to "taking that which one cannot or will not internalize or accept and casting that characteristic onto another person, place, or thing." Clearly, Western cultures have projected such strong negative images on sharks that myth has obscured fact.

Marine naturalist, artist, and author Richard Ellis commented on the phenomenon this way: "We 'advanced' folk of the late twentieth century probably think of ourselves as being beyond pagan mysticism; in fact we are in the grip of an even stronger mythology. We have elevated the shark to a position in our pantheon that transcends that of any other animal. Only the whale has achieved a comparable mythification; but there we have fabricated a benevolent spirit, a spirit contrasted with the shark as the embodiment of evil, the representative of the underworld."

This viewpoint is clearly evident after those rare incidents of shark attack and even when large sharks are caught by fishermen or put on exhibit at marine aquaria. Large, bold-print newspaper headlines appear as front-page attention grabbers, and television "news" crews purportedly cover the story from many angles, but in almost all cases, the focus seems to be the mythic menace of sharks.

Of course, scientists who study sharks and professional divers who spend time with sharks in natural settings do not subscribe to the myth, so it is not really a barrier to important efforts to understand the shark. In fact, even highly sensationalistic books and films about sharks have, in some ways, had a positive effect, making more and more people aware of sharks and helping to spur avid naturalists to champion the cause of protecting the marine environment and shark populations in many areas around the world.

It seems to me that the more things that are done to keep sharks prominent in the public eye, the less chance there is that educated, caring people will allow sharks to be overfished and threatened with extinction. I am not certain that such a policy is the intent of all those who help to create a more informed Western perception of sharks, but I do think it is a very valuable by-product.

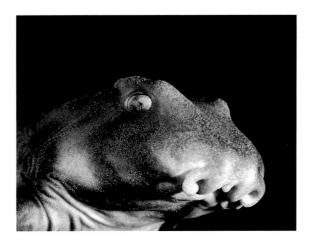

NOT ALL SHARKS LOOK LIKE HOLLYWOOD'S VERSION OF JAWS. THIS HORN

SHARK IS NOT LIKELY TO FRIGHTEN TODAY'S SOPHISTICATED MOVIEGOERS, BUT IT IS WELL

EQUIPPED FOR ITS ROLE AS A PREDATOR IN CALIFORNIA REEF COMMUNITIES.

ABOVE: IN A NEPTUNIC ANTISHARK SUIT, HOWARD HALL, A FILMMAKER, SHOOTS FOOTAGE FOR A TELEVISION SHOW. SHARKS
AND OTHER POTENTIALLY DANGEROUS ANIMALS WITH SHARP TEETH OFTEN TRANSLATE TO HIGH TELEVISION RATINGS.

⋟

INSET: LIKE SHARKS, MORAY EELS HAVE LONG BEEN DEPICTED IN LITERATURE, MYTHOLOGY, AND IN FILMS AS BEING VICIOUS
SEA MONSTERS. THAT IMAGE SERVES HOLLYWOOD WELL, BUT EXPERIENCED DIVERS KNOW EELS TO BE SHY AND RECLUSIVE.

LEFT: DIVER CHIP MATHESON DEMONSTRATES THE STAINLESS-STEEL CHAIN-MESH NEPTUNIC ANTISHARK SUIT AS HE GETS BITTEN BY A BLUE SHARK. SCENES LIKE THIS ONE HAVE BEEN FEATURED ON MANY TELEVISION SHOWS ABOUT SHARKS, BUT IF NOT WISELY HANDLED, SUCH IMAGES HELP SPREAD THE MYTH OF SHARKS AS INDISCRIMINATE KILLING MACHINES.

❧

BELOW: KILLER WHALES (THEIR FINS SHOWN HERE), LIKE BARRACUDAS, GIANT SQUID, SEA SNAKES, AND OF COURSE SHARKS HAVE LONG BEEN PORTRAYED AS EVIL, MAN-EATING MONSTERS.

ABOVE: SHARKS INHABIT ALMOST ALL OCEANIC ZONES, FROM CLEAR, SHALLOW CORAL REEF
COMMUNITIES TO TEMPERATE KELP FORESTS TO SUBPOLAR SEAS. SOME SHARKS LIVE NEAR THE
SURFACE, AND OTHERS SPEND THEIR LIVES THOUSANDS OF FEET BELOW.

❧

RIGHT: A VARIETY OF REEF SHARKS SUCH AS THE WHITETIP HAVE LONG BEEN REVERED, EVEN
WORSHIPPED, BY AFRICAN TRIBESMEN AND SOUTH PACIFIC ISLANDERS.

ABOVE: SURPRISING TO MANY, APPROXIMATELY 80 PERCENT OF ALL FULL-GROWN SHARKS ARE SMALLER THAN ADULT

HUMANS. THIS NEWBORN HORN SHARK WILL REACH A MAXIMUM LENGTH OF ONLY 3.5 TO 4 FEET (1 TO 1.22 M).

❧

BELOW: REFERRED TO AS DEVILFISH, MANTA RAYS WERE ONCE CONSIDERED TO BE EXTREMELY DANGEROUS TO HUMANS. EXPERIENCED DIVERS KNOW BETTER.

NATURAL HISTORY

LAYMEN OFTEN SPEAK ABOUT SHARKS AS IF
there is only one species, as if all sharks are the same. This commonly accepted mis-
conception is a long way from the truth. Worldwide, there are more than 350
species (some sources say up to 370), which differ significantly in a wide variety of
ways. Understanding how various species of shark differ provides an insight into
the unique place of each species in nature's overall plan.

Some species, such as the mako shark, prey primarily on fish; others, such as the
great white shark, feed mostly on marine mammals. Horn sharks, nurse sharks,
swell sharks, and leopard sharks crush a variety of crustaceans – lobsters, shrimp,
and crabs – as well as mollusks, a grouping that includes octopuses, snails, and
conchs. Sea turtles are a favorite prey of tiger sharks and some other species that
inhabit tropical-reef communities.

Blue sharks prey on squid and a wide variety of small schooling fish, and the
great whale shark, the largest fish in the sea, feeds on dense concentrations of tiny

LEFT: A SHARK IN THE WILD MAY BE IDENTIFIED BY OVERALL BODY SHAPE. THE BLUE SHARK PICTURED HERE IS

SLEEK AND SLENDER. MANY OTHER SPECIES APPEAR MORE MUSCULAR AND HEAVIER.

planktonic organisms and some small fish. Many sharks are primarily nocturnal hunters, but many are also described as opportunistic feeders, animals that readily feed during day or night, whenever a chance presents itself.

One characteristic that helps distinguish among the various species of shark is their teeth, which vary according to preferred prey. Often used for crushing, the teeth of tiger sharks and some other reef dwellers are shorter and broader than the teeth of fish eaters, such as mako sharks. The sharply pointed teeth of makos are long and narrow and are often referred to as "fish teeth." The mako does not need serrated teeth like those the great white uses to rip the flesh from large marine mammals, but instead needs teeth that can pin fast-moving fish such as tuna, mackerel, and even billfish. Some species, such as horn sharks and Port Jackson sharks, have teeth that are specialized for crushing.

Perhaps the most basic thing that all species of shark share is the fact that they are types of fish. Scientists separate fish into broad categories, depending upon whether the fish's skeleton is made of bone, as are those of grouper, angelfish, barracuda, tuna, and billfish, or of cartilage, as are those of all sharks, rays, and skates.

Sharks, rays, and skates differ from bony fish in a number of significant ways:

- Scales: Cartilaginous fish (sharks, rays, and skates) lack the true scales of bony fish, which are typically large, rounded, and bonelike, but do have dermal denticles, which are modified, toothlike structures.
- Gill Covers: Whereas bony fish typically have one gill cover – the bonelike operculum, used to pump oxygenated water through the gills – on each side of the head, sharks, rays, and skates have five to seven paired uncovered gill slits on each side of the head.

- Swim Bladder: Sharks, rays, and skates do not have the gas-filled organ that provides bony fish with buoyancy.
- Method of Reproduction: Most species of cartilaginous fish copulate and the young are born live (although there are many exceptions to this). Bony fish typically spawn, the young hatching from eggs.
- Mouth Position: In most species of cartilaginous fish, the mouth is underslung, positioned under the snout; however, the mouths of some species, like those of all bony fish, are in the terminal position, that is, at the forwardmost position of the head.
- Tail Shape and Location: With some notable exceptions, the tails of sharks, rays, and skates are asymmetrical and are positioned where the vertebrae end. The tails of bony fish are usually symmetrical and are extensions of the backbone.
- Tooth Attachment: The teeth of sharks, rays, and skates are not firmly affixed to the jaw, whereas those of bony fish are attached to jaw sockets.

Generally speaking, though they may aggregate in the same general area, sharks are solitary. Even members of the same species are considered to be competitors more than partners in any form of cooperative social behavior. Scalloped hammerheads do live together in large schools often containing as many as several hundred individuals; however, cooperation among them is not documented or even suspected. These 6- to 12-foot (2- to 4-m)-long sharks gather together at prominent undersea landmarks such as seamounts – underwater mountains – during the day, but spread out to hunt by themselves at night. During these nocturnal ventures, scalloped hammerheads often swim as far as 15 miles (24 km) away from their daytime gathering sites, but they manage to navigate back to join the school by the break of day.

Sharks also differ significantly in size and shape. At one end of the range, whale sharks can be up to 50 feet (15 m) long and weigh 30,000 to 50,000 pounds (13,500 to 22,500 kg). In contrast, full-grown pygmy sharks are a mere 6 to 9 inches (15 to 23 cm) long and weigh between 1 and 2 pounds (0.5 to 0.9 kg).

Typically, sharks have an elongated, torpedo-shaped body that is thicker toward the front end and narrower toward the tail. The upper portion, or lobe, of the tail of most species is larger than the lower lobe, but white sharks, mako sharks, porbeagles, and salmon sharks are exceptions as their tails are almost symmetrical. The tail provides thrust, while the paired pectoral fins fused to the body near the head and gills are used for maneuverability.

But there are plenty of exceptions to the stereotypical shape. Eight species of hammerhead shark have greatly flattened, winglike heads, which provide lift at the front of the body to aid swimming. The hammerhead design also spreads sensory organs in the head farther apart, enabling these sharks, in theory, to locate potential predators and prey more quickly. When searching the bottom for prey that might be buried in the substrate, hammerheads often swing their heads back and forth across their path in an effort to detect prey. The widened head helps them expand the search pattern. Angel sharks, sand sharks, and carpet sharks, or wobbegongs, are also exceptions; their bodies are much flatter than the stereotypical design.

Another way in which sharks vary is in their method of giving birth. As is the case for all cartilaginous fish, the males impregnate females by means of internal fertilization. Each male has a pair of tube-shaped claspers, located on the underbelly close to the tail. During mating, the male inserts one of the claspers into the body of the female and delivers sperm through it.

26

Fertilization is the same in all species of sharks, but giving birth varies significantly. Blue sharks, silky sharks, and lemon sharks bear live young; however, horn sharks and swell sharks lay eggs, usually on the sea floor or on soft coral, to which they are attached by tough, curly, fibrous threads, or wedge the eggs into cracks or crevices in the reef. It can take longer than a year for the eggs of some species to hatch.

Great white, tiger, and a variety of other sharks are described as intrauterine cannibals – that is, inside the mother, the most capable young devour their brothers and sisters, or eat unhatched eggs. When no more food remains inside the mother, the young are released into the wild. It is suspected that in most cases, two young are produced, one from each of two uterine canals – part of the reproductive system.

Litter sizes vary from one or two to as many as 200 in some rare instances in blue sharks. However, blue sharks most commonly produce several dozen young.

As far as parental care is concerned, the best the young can hope for is not to be eaten by either of their parents. In other words, once sharks are born, they are strictly on their own, fair game for any creature capable of capturing them. It is suspected that nature attempts to improve the odds in favor of the young's survival by diminishing the appetite of the female who has just delivered. Although this theory holds for many species, field observation of the gray reef sharks makes it suspect.

In many species, gravid females move away from the general area inhabited by the rest of the mature population in order to deliver their young and join up with other gravid females. For example, scalloped hammerheads, which as adults inhabit the open sea, are born in shallow coastal estuaries and bays. Lemon sharks are typically born in shallow sand flats, where they spend the early part of their lives before moving out to the deeper surrounding waters.

Many sharks are surprisingly long-lived. Ten years might be considered a significant life span in some species, but great whites are commonly believed to live to be 30 to 35 years old in the wild. Probably the most studied shark population in the world is that of the lemon sharks in and around the isle of Bimini in the Bahamas. Teams of researchers led by Dr. Sonny Gruber have determined that lemon sharks live to be at least 75 years old in natural settings, and that they might live as long as 125 years.

This ability to survive for so many years leads many to wonder about the intelligence of sharks. While the commonly accepted view is that sharks are not particularly intelligent creatures, their relative longevity suggests that they are certainly more capable of dealing with the problems posed by their environment than are many animals.

THE EVOLUTION OF SHARKS

Most specialists agree that in one form or another, sharks have roamed earth's waters for at least 450 million years. To put that figure into perspective, the fossil record of sharks is three times longer than that of the dinosaurs, and more than 100 times that of humans: it reaches back to before the first vertebrates crawled out of the sea onto land, prior to the existence of insects, and even before many plants had taken root on major continents.

That is not to say, however, that any species of shark has been extant for that length of time. The oldest fossils that paleontologists identify with a currently living group of sharks date back approximately 180 million years, and the ancestry of most modern species can be traced back only for 100 to 120 million years.

In most instances, the fossil record consists primarily of teeth, but in exceptional cases complete skeletons have been discovered. Since the skeleton of both ancient and modern-day sharks is made of cartilage, which decomposes quickly after death and is not as easily fossilized as bone, intact fossilized sharks are rarely discovered. Shark teeth, on the other hand, contain significant amounts of calcium phosphate, and readily fossilize. Sharks constantly shed old teeth and grow new ones; over the course of a lifetime many sharks discard tens of thousands of teeth. As a result, fossilized sharks' teeth are commonly found in many parts of the world.

For some reason, many people consider the sharks, rays, and skates to be inferior to bony fish. This assumption is unfounded. In fact, cartilage provides some advantages to bone. Cartilage is almost weightless in water, and as a result the cartilaginous fish does not need a gas bladder to compensate for the weight of its skeleton. Whereas most bony fish are confined to a limited depth range and, when they stray outside it, must either ascend or descend slowly to adjust for pressure changes and the expansion or contraction of gases in the gas bladder, a shark is free to swim from the sea floor to the surface and back again at whatever speed it chooses.

One of the oldest and most primitive of all shark species is the *Cladoselache*; 400 million years ago, these sharks inhabited the waters of a shallow ocean basin that extended over much of what we now know as the North American continent. Strange as it may seem, fossil evidence of this shark is well documented in the rocks of the Paleozoic strata in inland states such as Ohio, Tennessee, and Kentucky. Equipped with a long, thin jaw and rather stiff, triangular fins, which were supported by rows of cartilage, *Cladoselache* attained a length of just over 3 feet (1 m). Well-preserved fossils, complete with prey swallowed tail first, indicate that *Cladoselache* was a fish eater. Several pointed cusps were present on the teeth; however, the cusps in fossilized teeth often appear shortened and worn down, suggesting that *Cladoselache* did not replace its teeth as modern sharks do.

Its large powerful tail, which was similar in structure to the symmetrical tail of modern-day mako sharks and great white sharks, is indicative of the fact that *Cladoselache* was probably a fast swimmer, a skill that was necessary to avoid predation by the huge armored fish of that era.

Only in recent years have scientists begun to gain a fundamental understanding of many other sharks that existed long ago, during the Paleozoic era. Some of those creatures possessed armorlike spines that projected outward from their dorsal fin, but in some species it appears that only the males were so armed. In some, these spines curved forward in bizarre fashion, helping to protect the head. Other species became equipped with spiral-shaped teeth exposed under their chin. Scientists believe that approximately 350 million years ago, a variety of species began to evolve into forms that are the ancestors of modern-day rabbitfish (chimaeras).

Interestingly, after this period of diversification, there was an extended period of "evolutionary stasis." From approximately 300 million to 150 million years ago, it appears that only two major groups of sharks existed. One group, the xenacanths, almost exclusively inhabited fresh-water environs. These sharks were widespread from 450 million years ago until their mysterious extinction approximately 220 million years ago.

The second group, the hybodonts, appeared approximately 320 million years ago. These sharks dominated both salt- and fresh-water environments until they eventually were forced out by competition from modern-day species. The hybodonts became extinct at approximately the same time the dinosaurs did, and fossil records of both can be found in Wyoming in the strata from the Upper Crustaceous Era.

The earliest evidence of currently living species is the fossilized teeth of mako sharks, which have been well documented from the Lower Crustaceous Era, some 100 million years ago. Fossil remains of the modern-day great white date back approximately 65 million years. The rise of the large, modern-day predators coincides with both the diversification of mammals, which are obvious food sources for the sharks, and the demise of competition from the dinosaurs. Certainly, wherever fossilized teeth from big, predatory sharks are found, paleontologists also discover an abundance of remains from seals, sea lions, dolphins, and whales. The bones of these suspected prey often show evidence of having been chewed on by sharks.

One behemoth that existed between 10 million and 25 million years ago was a species known as *Carcharodon megalodon*, which reached a length of close to 40 feet (12 m). Its serrated, triangular teeth were in excess of 7 inches (18 cm) long. By comparison, the longest tooth of a modern-day great white extends only slightly beyond 2 inches (5 cm). It is often assumed and widely believed that *Carcharodon megalodon* was the direct ancestor of the modern-day great white shark, but scientific evidence to support this hypothesis is lacking.

Specialists maintain that the hammerhead shark first appeared during the modern era. The winglike shape of its head is considered to be a natural experiment in design.

MODERN-DAY SHARKS

The 350-plus species of modern-day shark are described in eight scientific orders that contain 30 families. As they do all plants and animals, taxonomists classify sharks according to shared and unshared characteristics. Sharks described as being the same genus are the most closely related, while those in the same family are more closely related to one another than to species in other families within the same order. A general description of the shared characteristics of each order, as well as a list of the families described within the various orders, is outlined below. (Note that the number of species in any given order or family is approximate. Previously unknown species of shark are still being discovered on a regular basis, and long-known species are constantly being reclassified. If you check the figures in a variety of reference sources, you may well find conflicting data.)

Order Squatiniformes

Family *Squatinidae*   angel sharks

Typified by the Pacific angel shark, the sharks in this order are characterized by their flattened bodies, which have a "raylike" appearance. There are approximately 13 species in the order, and most reach a maximum length of 4 to 6 feet (1 to 2 m). All are ovoviviparous livebearers, meaning they produce shelled eggs that develop and hatch inside the body of the mother, but there is no placental connection between mother and young.

Order Pristiophoriformes

Family *Pristiophoridae*   sawsharks

There are approximately five species in this order, and all are described within a single family commonly known as the sawsharks. While the sawsharks' flat, bladelike snout armed with sharp, lateral teeth gives them the appearance of ferocity, these sharks are thought to be rather harmless. Their snouts are probably used to stun and disable prey. All sawsharks are ovoviviparous livebearers.

Order Squaliformes

Family *Squalidae*	dogfish sharks
Family *Oxynotidae*	roughsharks
Family *Echinorhinidae*	bramble sharks

Described in three families consisting of approximately 82 species in total, this order comprises a large and varied group of sharks. They occur in all oceans, and some live in water as deep as 20,000 feet (6 km). These sharks are characterized by their slender, cylinder-shaped bodies; the two dorsal fins, which are often equipped with spines; the lack of an anal fin; and comparatively long snouts with shortened mouths. Some have powerful teeth used for cutting only in the lower jaw, and others have such teeth in both jaws. All are ovoviviparous livebearers. Several of the approximately 73 species of dogfish shark are extremely valuable to commercial fisheries.

Order Hexanchiformes

Family *Chlamydoselachidae*	frilled sharks
Family *Hexanchidae*	six-gilled and seven-gilled sharks

Characterized by either six or seven pairs of gill slits as opposed to the five pairs found in other sharks; a single, spineless dorsal fin; and the lack of an anal fin, this small order consists of two families and approximately five species. Having worldwide distribution, the sharks in this order typically inhabit deep water. All are ovoviviparous livebearers.

Order Carcharhiniformes

Family *Proscylliidae*	finback catsharks
Family *Sphyrnidae*	hammerhead sharks
Family *Hemigaleidae*	weasel sharks
Family *Scyliorhinidae*	catsharks
Family *Pseudotriakidae*	false catsharks
Family *Triakidae*	houndsharks
Family *Leptochariidae*	barbled houndsharks
Family *Carcharhinididae*	requiem sharks

This order contains more species, approximately 197, than all other orders of shark combined. Some, like the catshark, are mostly small and inactive, while others, like the oceanic whitetip, blue, and hammerhead, are considered to be powerful, extremely active, open-ocean creatures. Many of the species commonly labeled as "dangerous to humans," such as the blue, oceanic whitetip, hammerhead, gray reef, silky, tiger, dusky, and bull shark, are part of this order. On the whole, they are extremely common in tropical seas, and quite common in temperate waters, especially in areas over continental shelves. However, some species in this order inhabit deep benthic waters and others surface waters of the open sea.

These sharks are characterized by their elongated snouts; comparatively long mouth, which extends forward of the eyes; the presence of an anal fin; and two dorsal fins, which lack spines. Their teeth vary from small and flattened to large and bladelike. They lack rear crushing teeth. In addition, the eyes of these sharks are protected by a movable, nictitating membrane, which is somewhat like a thickened eyelid. Rising from the bottom of the eye up, the nictitating membrane covers the eyes at the last moment when these sharks bite and feed. The species in this order reproduce in a wide variety of ways.

Order Orectolobiformes

Family *Orectolobidae*	wobbegongs
Family *Parascyllidae*	collared carpet sharks
Family *Brachaeluridae*	blind sharks
Family *Rhiniodontidae*	whale sharks
Family *Stegostomatidae*	zebra sharks
Family *Ginglymostomatidae*	nurse sharks
Family *Hemiscylliidae*	long-tailed carpet sharks

The sharks in this order belong to a relatively small but rather diverse group that comprises seven families and approximately 33 species. All are warm-water species that prefer shallow to moderate depths. Most occur in the tropical western Pacific, especially near Australia, but other species have a wider distribution. They are characterized by "piglike" snouts and short mouths, which in most species are linked directly to the nostrils by grooves. The nostrils are equipped with sensory barbels. These sharks possess an anal fin, and have two dorsal fins, which lack spines. Some species are oviparous, depositing eggs on the sea floor, while others are ovoviviparous livebearers.

Order Lamniformes

Family *Cetorhinidae*	basking sharks
Family *Mitsukurinidae*	goblin sharks
Family *Odontaspididae*	sand tiger sharks

Family *Megachasmidae*	megamouth sharks
Family *Pseudocarchariidae*	crocodile sharks
Family *Lamnidae*	mackerel sharks
Family *Alopiidae*	thresher sharks

Known as the mackerel sharks, this order comprises seven families and approximately 15 or 16 species. Some occur in all tropical, temperate, and subpolar seas. They are found in a wide variety of habitats, ranging from shallow intertidal depths to depths of 3,900 feet (1,190 m), and from the surf line of inshore waters to the center of huge oceanic basins.

Most are characterized by conical bodies, long snouts, and elongated mouths that extend behind the eyes. They possess an anal fin, and two spineless dorsal fins.

Classified as intrauterine cannibals, the embryonic sharks gain nutrition for an extended period before being released into the wild by feeding on either unhatched eggs or their newly hatched brothers and sisters inside the mother.

Order Heterodontiformes

| Family *Heterodontidae* | bullhead sharks |

This order consists of a single family comprising eight species. They are the only modern sharks that have spines on their anal fin as well as their two dorsal fins. All bullhead sharks are oviparous, meaning the females lay eggs. Some of the conical egg casings are equipped with threadlike fibers, while others have a screwlike shape to help keep them in place once they are planted.

THE DISTRIBUTION OF SHARKS

Sharks inhabit all of the world's oceans. Some bask on the surface of warm, clear tropical seas; others roam the depths of polar seas, where the water is icy cold and there is very little light. Some live in shallow nearshore waters, and many others inhabit the great expanses of the open sea. Some sharks prefer midwater, an area that is near neither the surface nor the sea floor. At least one modern species, the bull shark, is known to inhabit some fresh-water rivers, estuaries, and lakes.

The distribution of individual species can generally be defined in terms of water temperature, depth, activity level, and size, though these guidelines are not carved in stone. For example, mature great white sharks are typically found actively swimming in the relatively shallow water over continental shelves in temperate seas. Certainly there are exceptions, as white sharks are known to make open-ocean journeys and to inhabit tropical waters, but for the most part they prefer cooler waters where an abundance of marine mammals are found. Caribbean reef sharks, lemon sharks, gray reefs, whitetips, and silvertips inhabit some shallow reef communities of tropical seas, while oceanic whitetips and whale sharks roam open waters in tropical areas. Found in temperate seas around the world, blue sharks are often said to fill a niche in temperate seas that is similar to that occupied by oceanic whitetips in tropical oceans.

Active tropical sharks such as scalloped hammerheads, great hammerheads, silkies, duskies, bulls (also known as Zambezi), blacktips, and tiger sharks often travel considerable distances over the course of a day, and many undergo extensive seasonal migrations. At times, bull sharks are known to enter fresh-water rivers and lakes, and they have been documented as far as 1,800 miles (2,900 km) from the nearest ocean while swimming in the Amazon.

Most smaller tropical sharks, such as whitetip reef sharks, gray reef, blackspot, blacktip, and snaggletooth, tend to have smaller ranges than the larger species. Still smaller species, animals that attain a maximum size of approximately 3 feet (1 m), have an even smaller range and more limited distribution. Some occur only around a given island chain, or in one sector of a given sea. Their limited distribution is likely attributable to their small size and swimming capabilities. These species include a variety of houndsharks, sharpnose sharks, sicklefin weaselsharks, and hooktooth sharks.

Bottom-dwelling, tropical species, such as carpet sharks (also known as wobbegongs), banded catsharks, and several species of angel shark, tend to have limited distribution and small ranges. They are less active than most other tropical species, and tend to rest, well hidden, on the sea floor, awaiting the opportunity to surprise unsuspecting prey that inadvertently ventures too close. However, there are exceptions to this rule as well. The tawny nurse shark, the nurse shark (*Ginglymostoma cirratum*), and the zebra (sometimes called leopard) shark attain larger sizes, and have both larger areas of distribution and larger individual ranges. These species commonly reach lengths of 7 to 12 feet (2 to 4 m), and both the tawny nurse shark and the zebra shark can be found in reef communities throughout the Indo-Pacific.

It is interesting to note that several species of smaller tropical sharks populate reefs on both sides of the Central American land mass. Geologists suggest that the now separate populations were joined before the upheaval that created Central America.

As is the case with tropical sharks, temperate-water species are also either active swimmers or bottom dwellers. Active species, such as blue sharks, shortfin mako sharks, thresher sharks, great whites, sand tigers, and basking sharks, tend to follow major water currents as temperatures change over the course of a calendar year. During the winter months, these species move closer to the equator, and stray farther from it in summer, when water temperatures rise.

Interestingly, many of these species are found in both the Northern and Southern Hemispheres, but they are only rarely, if ever, encountered in between, in tropical seas. As a rule, when in the tropics, they inhabit deeper, cooler waters.

Blues undertake some of the longest known migrations. Individuals tagged in waters off New York have been recovered as far away as Spain and Brazil. And specimens tagged near San Diego, California, have been recovered only 36 hours later as far as 150 miles (240 km) away.

Smaller, though active temperate species, such as the spiny dogfish, Japanese dogfish, and soupfin, tend to have more limited distribution than larger species. The less active, bottom-dwelling sharks of temperate seas typically grow to less than 5 feet (1.5 m) in length. Their range tends to be limited, often in very restricted areas of a given sea, or around a particular archipelago. Angel sharks, sawsharks, some catsharks, and horn sharks also represent this group.

Several species of shark inhabit the chilly waters of subpolar regions, and a few species, such as the Greenland shark, have been reported under ice floes. Cowsharks, Portuguese sharks, frilled sharks, goblin sharks, some catsharks and false catsharks, some dogfish, as well as six-gilled and seven-gilled sharks are included in the grouping of cold-water species. Portuguese sharks have been caught in waters as deep as 5,000 feet (1,500 m). For many years, the larger, more active sharks that were known to inhabit cold waters were believed to be found only in polar and subpolar regions. However, in recent years, as more and more research is conducted, it has been discovered that many of these species occur worldwide.

When in temperate and even tropical seas, these sharks are found in the cold only at depths in excess of 1,000 feet (300 m). It is likely that "cold-water" sharks travel great distances because food is scarce in some cold-water sectors.

All of the smaller cold-water sharks are members of the dogfish family. They were once thought to be rather rare, but recent findings indicate that they are far more common than previously believed. The more than 30 species of bottom-dwelling, cold-water sharks, a group that includes deep-water catsharks and prickly sharks, are sedentary animals, traveling only short distances over the course of their lives. Some of these species are thought to occur in ranges measuring only a few thousand square miles.

THE BIOLOGY OF SHARKS

On the whole, sharks have not changed very much over the past 70 million years. This is probably partly because of the fundamental stability of their environment; however, the constancy of their physical characteristics speaks volumes about the excellence of design of their evolutionary ancestors. Having evolved from the placoderms, a group of rather primitive, jawed fish, early sharks were well on their way to becoming successful predators.

The bodies of species such as the gray reef, blue, mako, and silky are well designed for efficient swimming. A generic shark has a slender, streamlined body; elongated snout; relatively long pectoral fins; and tail whose upper lobe is larger than the lower. The front end of the body is slightly flattened in order to reduce friction when making sharp turns. The midbody is not as flattened and does experience slightly more drag than the forward end, providing a natural fulcrum against which to pivot when turning.

A typical shark swims by creating repeated sinuous motions with its body as its muscles emit transverse waves that are sent down the body. The lateral motion of the tail pushes the shark slightly downward through the water, but the pectoral fins counter this force by providing lift. Buoyancy is controlled with a minimal expenditure of energy. Their lightweight skeleton is made of cartilage, and their large oily livers keep the density of their bodies at a minimum. In water, a blue shark's weight is approximately 2.5 percent of what it weighs in air. This ratio is typical of many actively swimming sharks. In bottom-dwelling species, such as angel sharks, the in-water weight is closer to 6 percent of the in-air weight.

The skin of embryonic sharks develops from the mouth back, and in live sharks the skin is made of dermal denticles, which are actually modified teeth. Each denticle consists of a base plate and a sharpened pedicel. The denticles align in one direction, making a shark's skin feel sandpaper rough when rubbed in one direction and smooth as velvet when stroked in the other. It is believed that the rough skin actually creates less resistance when the shark moves through water than perfectly smooth skin would. The quiet laminar flow of water over the skin also helps make sharks hydro-dynamically quiet, a big advantage to a predator that uses stealth as part of its arsenal.

The tails of sharks provide significant insight into the lifestyle of individual species. The large upper lobe found in tiger sharks and hammerheads helps to provide power for cruising and for the rapid bursts of speed needed to catch fast-moving prey. The nearly symmetrical tail of makos, great whites, porbeagles, and salmon sharks is used primarily to provide the maximum speed when the shark is trying to chase down its preferred diet of fast-moving fish.

The tails of some bottom-dwelling species, such as nurse sharks and whitetip reef sharks, have an upper lobe that is much larger than the lower. These species prefer to prey on a variety of invertebrates that live in, on, or near the sea floor. With broad, slow, sweeping motions, the tail pushes the shark forward in a slightly head-down attitude, putting the sensory organs and mouth in just the right position to capture prey. Catsharks and carpet sharks, also bottom-dwelling species, swing the entire back end of their bodies for propulsion, not just the tail.

The tail of the thresher shark is almost as long as the rest of its body. It is believed that threshers swing their tails to herd and stun prey. The position of the eyes high atop the head complements this strategy.

It is interesting to note several adaptations that allow certain species to live more successful lives in their particular natural niches. For example, unlike most sharks, whose core body temperature is very close to that of the surrounding water, the core temperature of mako sharks and great whites is usually 5 to 11 degrees higher than the surrounding water. The elevated core temperature in these sharks provides them with faster and more efficient muscular responses.

The bodies of most sharks contain both red and white muscle tissue. Using the oxidation of fat to supply energy, red muscle tissue sustains long-term swimming. In contrast, white muscle tissue uses glycogen from sugar, and it is relied upon to supply rapid bursts of speed over a short period of time. Typically, the red muscle tissue is located in a thin layer just beneath the skin. However, in mako sharks, an interesting adaptation can be found: the red muscle tissue is found deep within the body, near the vertebral column. This tissue is linked to the circulatory system of mako sharks in order to work as a heat exchanger to reduce heat loss – an efficient design for a shark that needs to maintain a core temperature higher than the temperature of the surrounding water.

Another interesting adaptation is found in several bottom-dwelling species such as dogfish and goblin sharks, which live in deep water. Their body density is quite low compared with that of most other sharks, a characteristic that makes them almost neutrally buoyant. Because food is scarcer in deep waters, these species are probably very active swimmers, forced to cover a lot of territory in the quest for food. The less dense their bodies, the less energy they must expend when swimming.

As is the case with many of the oceans' larger creatures, whale sharks and basking sharks, the two largest species, have adapted to a lifestyle of feeding primarily upon plankton. Considering the fact that the biomass of plankton far exceeds that of fish or larger invertebrates, it is logical for big animals to prey on plankton.

An examination of shark jaws and teeth reveals even more fascinating adaptations. It is widely known that throughout their lives, sharks constantly produce new teeth. Teeth are aligned in rows; the forwardmost are used to bite, tear, and chew, while those behind are in line to move forward and replace teeth that wear out, break off, or are shed. The teeth are not embedded in the cartilage of the jaw, but instead are attached to a membrane known as the "tooth bed." The tooth bed is analogous to a conveyor belt, which moves forward in the process of replacing old teeth.

The jaws are not firmly fixed in the head of sharks the way those of humans and many large carnivores are. Instead, they are attached to a hinged tendon band that allows the protrusible jaws of sharks to extend well forward when the mouth is opened. As the mouth is opened, the teeth, especially those of the upper jaw, extend forward. A moment later, as the shark closes its mouth, the jaws and teeth fold inward, with the teeth pointing backward toward the stomach. This adaptation greatly assists sharks in capturing prey and pushing it toward the stomach.

Caribbean reef sharks, tiger, blues, makos, great whites, silkies, hammerheads, silvertips, and gray reefs, which often prey on animals that are too large to be consumed in a single bite, usually tilt their heads backward at the last instant as they approach their prey. In an ideal hit, the lower jaw makes first contact. Helping the shark to get a grip on its intended victim, the more spikelike teeth in the lower jaw are often longer and thinner than those of the upper jaw. After the lower jaw has been readied, the upper jaw and teeth move outward, up, and then down. The teeth of the upper jaw push into the prey, and the shark then moves its head back and forth in an effort to rip and saw the prey into manageable bite-sized portions.

Some bottom-dwelling species, such as nurse sharks, have another marvelous adaptation. They purse their lips together in such a way that when they open their mouths, they create powerful suction that dislodges a variety of invertebrates and small fish from their hiding places.

Sharks do not need to chew their food in order to begin the digestive process. Once they swallow the food, their stomach acids easily perform that task. A full meal is generally thought to take about 24 to 124 hours to digest. And contrary to the popularly accepted myth, sharks often go a number of days, and even weeks on end, without feeding.

On the whole, the growth rate of sharks is rather slow by comparison with that of many other animals, including most bony fish. This characteristic, combined with small litter sizes and long gestation periods, makes many species of shark highly susceptible to overexploitation.

Shark Senses

Exactly how sharks perceive the world around them, and precisely how and why various stimuli trigger specific reactions, are matters of much fascination and debate among laymen and experts alike. The most important concept to understand is that no one isolated sense but rather the integration of senses is what enables sharks to interpret and respond to stimuli as they do.

The senses of hearing and touch in sharks are elaborate, involving a number of specialized, hairlike cells positioned near the surface of the body. The majority of these cells are located in a series of pits, canals, and grooves that compose the sensitive sensory system known as the lateral line. This curved row of nerves branches in the front of the head and then extends down the side of the body into the tail. Mechanical stimulation received through pressure waves in the water sends nerve impulses to the central nervous system to be analyzed.

Studies have verified that sharks can detect both the direction and the intensity of movement, and the sheer number of nerve fibers in the lateral line suggest that they rely heavily upon this sensory system. It is well documented that many fish-eating species, such as gray reef and silky sharks, are attracted by low-frequency vibrations similar to those a struggling fish might make. In a number of studies, scientists have been able to attract sharks and to arouse them by emitting low-frequency sounds in water. Though probably unaware of the existence of the lateral-line system, fishermen throughout remote regions of the South Pacific traditionally use submerged rattles to attract sharks.

Interestingly, the lateral-line system has a built-in protection, or blocking mechanism, that prevents a shark from overloading its own lateral line via its own movements.

Sharks do have inner ears, but the opening to the inner ear from the surface of the skin is very small. Many specialists suspect that the inner ear is used primarily for balance, not hearing, though studies have shown that hair cells within the inner ear are also stimulated by vibrations in the water.

On the whole, sharks have a very well developed sense of smell, a fact that has long been known by fishermen and anyone who has ever tried to bait sharks in order to take pictures. More than one spearfisherman has lost to a hungry shark a bleeding fish that was no longer struggling. The olfactory receptors are positioned on the shark's snout, while the gustatory, or taste, receptors are located in the mouth. Studies have shown that sharks are capable of detecting minute concentrations of chemicals in water (as low as one part per million), but just because a shark detects the presence of blood or some other stimulus does not mean it will act upon it. In other words, just because a shark smells blood in the water does not mean that an instantaneous and uncontrollable feeding frenzy will result. However, as the amount, or concentration, of meat or blood increases, the chance that a shark will bite nearby objects increases dramatically.

Some sharks have large, well-developed eyes; others do not seem to rely as heavily upon their sense of sight. On the whole, a shark's eyes are similar to those of many vertebrates. However, there is a significant difference between the eyes of animals that live on land and see through air, and those of sharks, which live in and see through water. The cornea, the transparent layer in the front of the eye, is denser than air but the same density as water. In most terrestrial vertebrates, the difference in density causes light rays that enter the eye to be bent, or refracted. This phenomenon helps the lens focus the light on sensitive cells in the retina. As a result, the lens in land vertebrates does not need to be very powerful and can be comparatively thin, allowing the animals to easily change their point of focus by changing the shape of the lens.

Sharks' corneas have the same density as the surrounding water; thus, the cornea cannot assist in focusing an image. That responsibility falls to the lens, which must be relatively large and powerful and therefore cannot easily change shape. To compensate for the fixed lens, sharks reposition it relative to the retina in order to focus the light rays, or image. However, some specialists suggest that the lens does not move enough to provide a razor-sharp image.

Suspended within the eyeball, the lens is normally held in a position that will provide optimum long-range vision, which suggests that most sharks use their eyes to gather information at long range and rely upon other senses at close range.

Sharks' retinas contain numerous specialized cells called rods, which function well in dim lighting conditions, and some cones, which perform best at high light levels. Studies conducted with lemon sharks verify that at least some species respond to color cues. Several species have also demonstrated the ability to distinguish between different shapes and light levels.

In a variety of highly publicized tests, many of which have been repeatedly shown or imitated on television, great white sharks and other species have been seen to be more likely to attack bright red, orange, and yellow objects than objects of darker colors. A number of noted specialists seriously question the validity of many of those tests since so many other factors, such as bait and boats, divers, and shark cages, were also present. However, after repeatedly seeing one spectacular shark attack after another on their television screens, many surfers have retired their "yum-yum" yellow wetsuits.

Comparatively inactive species such as horn sharks and wobbegongs have small eyes relative to their overall body size, suggesting that they rely upon senses other than vision in their daily lives. More active, predatory species, such as blue sharks, mako sharks, and tiger sharks, are equipped with larger eyes. Thresher sharks have extremely large eyes (up to one-fifth of their overall head size), a characteristic typical of deep-water predatory fish. Their eyes are positioned high atop the head, giving them an unobstructed look at their prey of small schooling fish, which they herd and stun with their tails.

One of the more remarkable features of shark eyes is a series of reflecting plates, called the tapetum lucidum, located slightly behind the retina. The tapetal plates work like natural mirrors, and they reflect as much as 90 percent of some colors back into the light-sensitive cells in the retina. This phenomenon significantly increases sharks' sensitivity to light, and it also makes some shark eyes glow in the dark, much like those of cats.

The tapetum lucidum of sharks that inhabit bright, shallow waters may darken when movable pigments prevent the eyes from being "overloaded" by too much light. The darkening process is analogous to partially closing the blinds over a window. Those species that permanently inhabit deep, dark waters lack the tapetal plates.

It is difficult to say exactly why so many people believe that sharks have relatively poor eyesight and rely upon their other senses. Perhaps that belief is based on the fact that sharks use a variety of other sensory adaptations as well, and some species are thought to rely more heavily on senses other than their vision when they are close to their prey. However, nature does not waste energy, and the creation and maintenance of any adaptation is energy-expensive. In other words, if sharks didn't rely on vision, they wouldn't possess such a remarkable variety of well-adapted eyes.

Sharks, like rays and skates, have a highly specialized ability to detect electrical fields. All living organisms emit an electrical field, and the ability to detect these fields gives sharks a big advantage in the competition between predator and prey. Experiments have shown that sharks can detect electrical currents that are 10,000 times fainter than those that can be detected by any other group of animals. In some studies, scientists completely buried electrodes in the sand and found that when baited sharks were attracted to the area, they often bit at the current-producing electrodes far more frequently and more aggressively than they did at actual bait.

This ability to detect electrical fields is probably used by some species as an aid in orientation and navigation. Experiments suggest that juvenile lemon sharks use their ability to detect slight anomalies in the earth's magnetic field to locate and remain within the safety of the shallow sand flats in Bimini, where their nursery areas are located. Larger sharks, including members of their own species, flourish in the deeper waters bordering the nurseries, and these large sharks pose a considerable threat to a small lemon shark.

As with other cartilaginous fish, juvenile lemon sharks create their own electrical field as they swim in a given direction. The field is altered by the earth's magnetic field as the sharks swim. The shark's ability to measure and respond to small deviations allows it to use this sense as a method of navigating and orienting.

It is also believed that scalloped hammerheads use their ability to detect variations in the earth's magnetic field to find their way back to the seamounts where they gather during the day. At night, these sharks spread out and hunt as solitary animals, often traveling as far as 15 miles (24 km) from the prominent seamounts. In many locations, their night-time journeys take them over areas where the sea floor is extremely deep, meaning that the sharks cannot rely on visual "landmarks" as clues for finding their gathering place at night's end. For years, specialists were baffled by the hammerheads' ability to find their way "home," but recent studies have suggested that navigation by means of the earth's electromagnetic fields is likely the key.

Located in the snout and head, the electroreceptors are called ampullae of Lorenzini. These small, gel-filled pits are connected to each other via pores in the shark's skin. Upon close examination of the head of a shark, it is possible to see individual organs that look like pinhead-sized dots.

ABOVE: HORN SHARKS ARE SO NAMED FOR THE HORNLIKE RIDGE ABOVE THEIR EYES AND FOR THE MODIFIED

SPINELIKE DERMAL DENTICLE NEXT TO THE DORSAL FIN.

৯

LEFT: SHARKS GAIN THEIR THRUST FROM THEIR LONG, POWERFUL TAIL FINS, AND USE THEIR PECTORAL FINS TO

PROVIDE LIFT AND TO MANEUVER.

ABOVE RIGHT: SMALL REEF FISH, SUCH AS THE SOLDIERFISH PICTURED HERE,
ARE FAVORITE FOOD SOURCES FOR MANY REEF SHARKS.

೩

BELOW RIGHT: ONE- TO 2-INCH-LONG (2.5–5 CM) TUNA CRABS ARE READILY
EATEN BY BLUE SHARKS, THOUGH THE CRABS ARE NOT THEIR TYPICAL DIET.
OPPORTUNISTIC FEEDING IS QUITE COMMON IN MANY SPECIES OF SHARK.

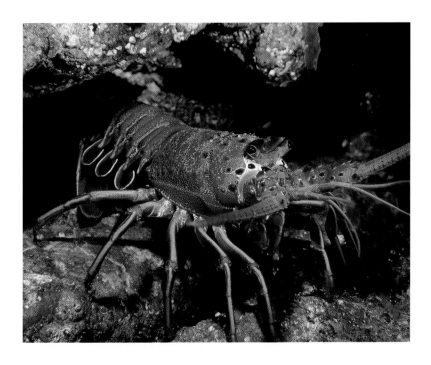

ABOVE LEFT: MANY SPECIES OF SHARK THAT EITHER LIVE ON OR HUNT NEAR THE SEA FLOOR ARE KNOWN TO PREY ON LOBSTERS AND THEIR CLOSE RELATIVES, THE SHRIMPS AND CRABS.

❧

BELOW LEFT: AS SHARP AND FORMIDABLE AS SEA URCHIN SPINES SEEM TO BE, THESE ECHINODERMS ARE READILY PREYED ON BY A VARIETY OF SHARKS.

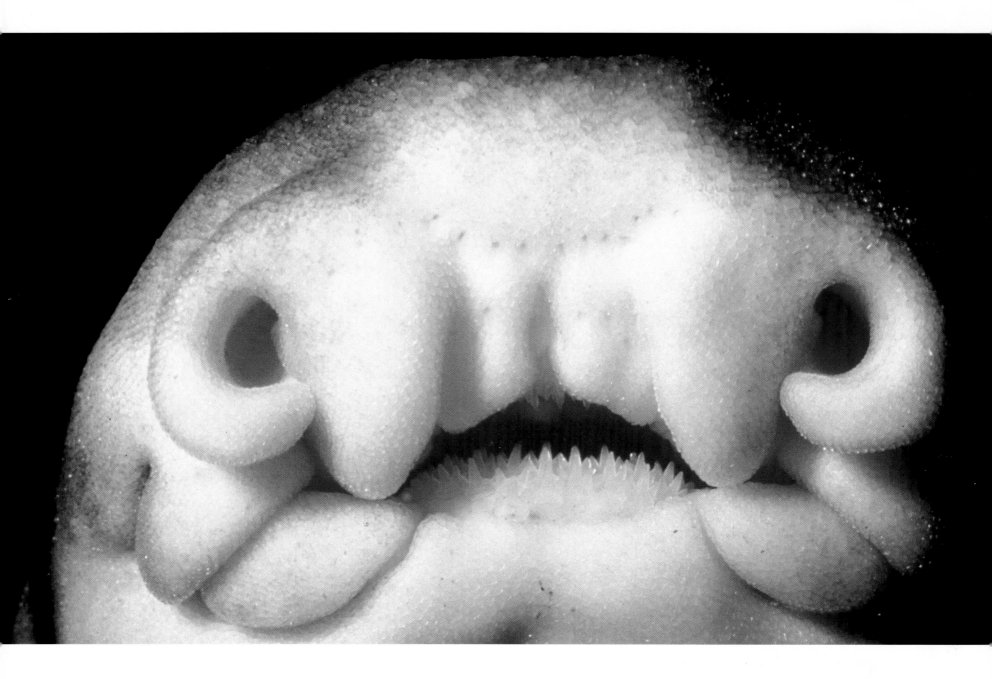

HORN SHARKS FEED ON ASSORTED BOTTOM DWELLERS SUCH AS SNAILS, CRABS, SHRIMP, AND LOBSTER. THEIR FRONT TEETH ARE EQUIPPED FOR GRABBING PREY, AND THOSE AT

THE BACK OF THE JAWS ARE FOR CRUSHING.

ABOVE: EVEN COMPARATIVELY SMALL SPECIES LIKE SWELL SHARKS AND LEOPARD SHARKS ARE

WELL EQUIPPED WITH ROWS OF REPLACEABLE RAZOR-SHARP TEETH.

❧

RIGHT: THE FOSSILIZED TOOTH, HELD IN A MAN'S HAND, ONCE BELONGED TO A SHARK KNOWN AS

CARCHARODON MEGALODON. THE SMALLER, WHITE, 2-INCH-LONG (5 CM) TOOTH BELONGS TO A

MODERN-DAY GREAT WHITE SHARK. THE ONCE-BELIEVED THEORY THAT THE GREAT WHITE IS A

DIRECT DESCENDANT OF THAT EXTINCT SHARK IS NO LONGER WIDELY ACCEPTED.

LEFT: THE MARKET, OR COMMON, SQUID PICTURED HERE ARE MATING. HUGE GATHERINGS OF MATING SQUID, CALLED RUNS, ATTRACT PREDATORS THAT RANGE FROM BLUE SHARKS, PILOT WHALES, BAT RAYS, AND SEA LIONS TO HORN SHARKS, ANGEL SHARKS, GUITARFISH, SCULPIN, AND LOBSTERS.

❧

BELOW: MOST SHARKS, LIKE THE CARIBBEAN REEF SHARK PICTURED HERE, HAVE FIVE PAIRS OF GILL SLITS, WHICH ARE POSITIONED ON THE SIDES OF THE HEAD.

OPPOSITE PAGE: DESPITE ALL THEIR WELL-PUBLICIZED AQUATIC SKILLS, DOLPHINS, ESPECIALLY YOUNGSTERS, ARE SUBJECT TO ATTACK FROM LARGE SHARKS. LIVING TOGETHER IN GROUPS KNOWN AS PODS, EXTENDED DOLPHIN FAMILIES HELP TO PROTECT ONE ANOTHER.

❧

OPPOSITE PAGE (INSET): SEA TURTLES ARE A FAVORITE PREY OF TIGER SHARKS AND SEVERAL OTHER SPECIES. IT TAKES SHARP TEETH AND POWERFUL JAWS TO RIP THROUGH AND CRUSH THEIR SHELLS.

ABOVE: THE ZEBRA SHARK HAS A TAIL ALMOST HALF AS LONG AS THE REST OF ITS BODY. THRESHER SHARKS ARE THE ONLY SHARKS WITH PROPORTIONATELY LONGER TAILS.

❧

ABOVE (INSET): A CLEANER WRASSE (BLUE FISH NEAR THE HEAD OF THIS ZEBRA SHARK) PROVIDES CLEANING SERVICE, RIDDING THE SHARK OF UNWANTED PARASITES. THE SHARK WILL LEAVE THE WRASSE UNHARMED.

ABOVE: REMORAS OFTEN ACCOMPANY SHARKS, OTHER FISH, DOLPHINS, TURTLES, AND OTHER MARINE ANIMALS. THE RELATION-

SHIP BETWEEN A REMORA AND ITS HOST IS NOT COMPLETELY UNDERSTOOD, BUT IT IS KNOWN THAT THE REMORAS HELP RID THE HOSTS OF SKIN PARASITES.

❧

BELOW: WHEN BLUE SHARKS, AND OTHER REQUIEM SHARKS, OPEN THEIR MOUTHS TO FEED, PROTECTIVE MEMBRANES KNOWN AS

NICTITATING MEMBRANES RAISE TO COVER THE EYES.

KILLER WHALES ARE KNOWN TO PREY ON A VARIETY OF SPECIES OF

SHARK. IT IS UNLIKELY THAT EVEN A LARGE SHARK WOULD BE MUCH

OF A MATCH FOR A FULL-GROWN KILLER WHALE.

RIGHT: THE ROW OF SMALL SPOTS OR DOTS FORWARD OF THE MOUTH OF THIS HAMMERHEAD SHARK ARE ORGANS KNOWN AS AMPULLAE OF LORENZINI. THESE HIGHLY SPECIALIZED SENSORY RECEPTORS ENABLE SHARKS TO DETECT FAINT ELECTRICAL FIELDS.

❧

BELOW: MANY TYPES OF OCTOPUSES ARE COMMONLY FOUND IN STOMACH-CONTENT ANALYSES OF SHARKS.

❧

BELOW RIGHT: FLATFISH LIKE THIS FLOUNDER ATTEMPT TO AVOID PREDATION BY BURYING THEMSELVES IN THE SAND, OR BY ALTERING THEIR COLOR AND PATTERN TO BLEND IN WITH THEIR SURROUNDINGS. IF DETECTED, HOWEVER, THEY WILL BE READILY EATEN BY VARIOUS KINDS OF SHARKS.

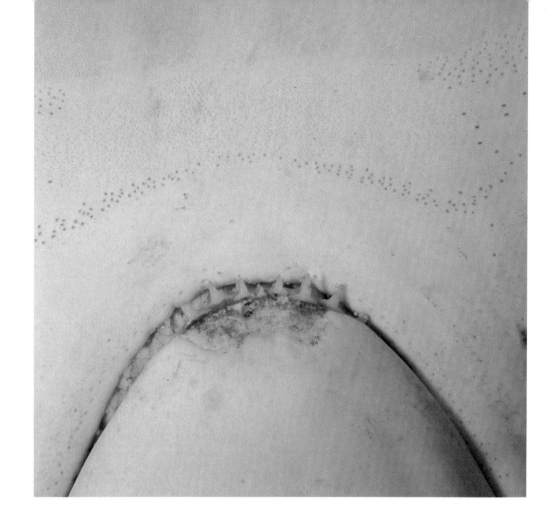

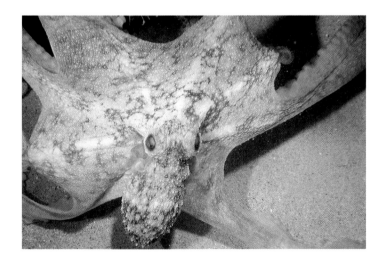

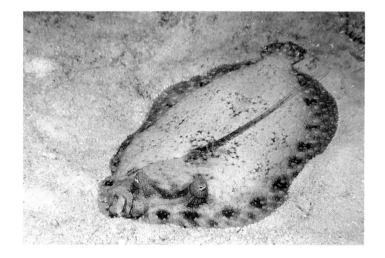

ABOVE: IN CARIBBEAN WATERS, REEF SQUID PROVE TO BE A VALUABLE FOOD SOURCE FOR

SHARKS AS WELL AS OTHER FISH.

❧

RIGHT: DESPITE THEIR SPEED AND AGILITY, JACKS ARE AN IMPORTANT FOOD SOURCE FOR

CERTAIN FAST-SWIMMING SHARKS.

SHARKS FEED ON MANY TYPES OF PREY –
PLANKTON, FISH, OCTOPUSES, SQUID,
SHELLFISH, MARINE MAMMALS, SEA BIRDS, AND
OTHER SHARKS, JUST TO NAME A FEW. HERE, A
WHITETIP REEF SHARK, A SPECIES THAT EATS
FISH AND A VARIETY OF ANIMALS THAT LIVE
NEAR THE SEA FLOOR, CRUISES THROUGH A
SCHOOL OF SNAPPERS IN THE WATERS OF
COSTA RICA'S COCOS ISLAND.

ALTHOUGH THERE ARE SOME NOTABLE EXCEPTIONS, THE TYPICAL SHARK TAIL IS ASYMMETRICAL, WITH THE UPPER LOBE LARGER THAN THE LOWER.

ABOVE: A TRIO OF WHITETIP REEF SHARKS RESTING ON THE SEA FLOOR,
PROVIDING PROOF THAT THOUGH SOME SHARKS SWIM ALL DAY EVERY DAY OF
THEIR LIVES, NOT ALL DO SO IN ORDER TO SURVIVE.

❧

LEFT: DESPITE SOME OBVIOUS DIFFERENCES IN FORM, SHARKS AND RAYS ARE
CLOSELY RELATED ANIMALS. THE SKELETONS OF SHARKS, RAYS, AND SKATES ARE
MADE OF CARTILAGE, AS OPPOSED TO BONE.

ABOVE: SOME, BUT CERTAINLY NOT ALL, SHARKS LAY EGGS. A SWELL SHARK INSIDE ITS EGG CASING.

ॐ

RIGHT: A TEAM OF SCIENTISTS LED BY DR. SONNY GRUBER OF THE UNIVERSITY OF MIAMI CONDUCTS A
GROWTH-STUDY EXPERIMENT ON A LEMON SHARK. IN NATURAL SETTINGS, LEMON SHARKS CAN LIVE
AT LEAST 75 YEARS, AND EVEN UP TO 125. BUT EVEN SO, MANY SHARKS DO NOT BEAR A LOT OF YOUNG
OVER THE COURSE OF A LIFETIME.

DESPITE THE FACT THAT BLUE SHARKS LIVE IN THE OPEN SEA, THEY ARE PRIMARILY SURFACE

DWELLERS. THIS IS A FEMALE BLUE.

ADVENTURES
IN THE WILD

EVERYWHERE I LOOKED I SAW SHARKS. THERE were at least 20, perhaps as many as 40. Missilelike silhouettes circled near the surface, while others cruised in the blue-black water below. As far as I could tell, all were blue sharks, but a few minutes earlier a big, heavy-bodied mako shark had appeared, swimming nervously. There was no time to stop and think. At that moment I realized that one of the larger sharks was swimming directly at me. I was pretty certain it was the same one that had bitten my left arm only moments earlier. I could still hear the grating noise the shark's teeth made as they raked across my arm.

The setting simply could not have been any better, and this had the potential to be the perfect moment. I raised my 16 mm movie camera to my eye, gently brushed away bubbles on the lens port that might distract from the scene, and framed my shot. I was about to film the climactic scene for a sequence in a film about blue sharks that was being produced for the television series *Mutual of Omaha's Wild Kingdom*.

LEFT: UP CLOSE AND PERSONAL! THAT'S OFTEN THE NATURE OF ENCOUNTERS WITH BLUE SHARKS OFF

SOUTHERN CALIFORNIA.

We were approximately 20 miles (32 km) straight out to sea from San Diego, exploring the waters of the open ocean. The water was warm, clear, and iridescent blue. A gentle breeze was working to help push our boat, the *Betsy M*, through the water and spread the odor corridor produced by the bait we had placed overboard only a few hours before.

I had been in similar situations many times before, and over the years I had come to truly love being out here, in the middle of nowhere, filming some of the most gorgeous creatures on earth. "Beautiful," "handsome," "stunning," and "graceful" are not the adjectives normally used to describe sharks, but to me they were apt, especially for blue sharks.

Blues are the most commonly encountered of the open-ocean sharks in the temperate waters off the coast of southern California. Despite the fact that blue sharks inhabit the open sea, they are not deep-water animals. Blue sharks live most of their lives in the top several hundred feet of water, swimming over bottoms that are thousands of feet deep. So named for their obvious blue coloration, they absolutely sparkle when shimmering rays of sunlight dance across their backs. Normally they glide gracefully, always appearing to be under complete control, attaining their forward thrust from their long, powerful tails, and maneuvering with their pectoral fins. While blues only rarely appear as if they are the slightest bit stressed, they are capable of great bursts of speed, and are often said to be among the fastest of all sharks.

The purpose of this segment of the show was to demonstrate the effectiveness of an antishark suit called the Neptunic. Cameraman Howard Hall and I were both wearing the stainless-steel antishark suits. Developed by Ron and Valerie Taylor from Australia and Jeremiah Sullivan from San Diego, the suit covers a diver from head to toe, with only a small opening for a mask and regulator. It is made of approximately 400,000 individually welded stainless-steel links, and for a 6-foot (1.8-m)-tall, 165-pound (75-kg) diver like me, a custom suit weighs about 17 pounds (8 kg). It is just about an even trade-off for my weight belt when I am wearing a ¼-inch (0.6-cm)-thick wetsuit made for diving in California water.

I had used my Neptunic on plenty of occasions, and wasn't even the slightest bit concerned about the grating noise the shark's teeth had made as they raked across my arm. After having been bitten a few hundred times, I had complete confidence in the suit's ability to keep me from suffering serious injury, at least from blue sharks. I certainly wouldn't want to test the suit against even a small great white shark.

Over the years I have come to realize that the odds of being attacked by a shark when there is no bait in the water are almost nil. But once you do bait in blue sharks – and a lot of other species, for that matter – the rules of the game change considerably. Rule number one is not to get between the bait and an oncoming shark, unless you are fully prepared for the encounter. Of course, that is usually exactly where a photographer wants to be. So, in the days before the invention of the anti-shark suit, we photographers picked our times carefully, and then moved in and out of the odor corridor created by the bait in order to get the shot and get out safely.

Before I ever tested the suit on my own body, I had seen it tested on cores of balsa wood wrapped in plastic bags filled with liquid dye that would spill out into the water in obvious clouds if cut, and I was quite confident that the suit was protection against serious injury. But, just the same, putting my arm inside a shark's mouth and hoping it would bite me for the camera was not something to be taken lightly. I wanted to get the in-the-flesh test over with as soon as possible, and the only thing this right-handed cameraman did as a hedge was offer the shark his left arm first.

Only on a few occasions have I ever really felt fear. One of the most notable was while filming blue sharks feeding on squid in the middle of a moonless winter night at Catalina Island near Los Angeles. Howard and I were filming for a *National Geographic* television special, and we thought we had ideal conditions. Common squid normally inhabit the open sea, but when they mate they gather in uncountable numbers over shallow bottoms. The squid are so intent upon mating that they are almost oblivious to anything going on around them.

Their presence attracts a host of predators and scavengers, including blue sharks, pilot whales, bat rays, harbor seals, elephant seals, and sea lions. The squid are attracted to bright lights, and they swarmed around our movie lights in such dense concentrations that it soon became impossible for Howard and me to see each other, even though we were easily within touching distance. In fact, we could not see through the squid to our lights, which were mounted on the end of the camera Howard was holding.

With all the squid gathered around us, we soon found ourselves in the center of the action. There were sharks darting about everywhere. All we could see was a passing shape and flashing teeth, and then, smack, one of us would get slammed by a shark – not bitten, but run into by a big blue shark that was stuffing itself full of squid. The action was so intense that Howard and I could not signal each other that we wanted to abort the dive. Each of us wanted out, but each of us thought he was demonstrating professional cool by waiting for the other guy to beg off first. After a few minutes, we ditched the lights, which were connected to the boat by a cable. As the lights sank slowly toward the bottom, we could see the silhouettes of at least a dozen blue sharks following them in the glow.

Back on board, we re-evaluated our techniques and were soon able to get back into the water, where we safely filmed a great sequence.

About 10 years ago, after many people had asked us about the possibility, Bob Cranston and I began to operate a business through See & Sea Travel in San Francisco, taking sport divers out off the coast of San Diego to observe and film blue sharks and mako sharks. Carl Roessler, the owner of See & Sea, had been taking selected clientele to Australia to see and film great white sharks for years, and we thought our experiences would serve as a great introduction for the action down under. Putting on a performance with the antishark suit was part of the show, but the thing I really enjoyed was seeing firsthand how people's impressions of sharks changed. I don't care who you are, if you have any imagination and you own a television set, there are shark myths at work in your brain. Separating fact from fiction is difficult, even for those of us who have spent a lot of time with sharks.

When Bob and I ran our trips, it gave us a lot of pleasure to hear people who we knew were scared before their first cage dive talking so excitedly after their dive about how beautiful sharks are. Of course, a dive or two later, they always wanted one of us to demonstrate the antishark suit on the biggest shark of the day.

The ultimate shark encounter in the minds of many divers is traveling to the Spencer Gulf in South Australia to come face to face with a great white shark. Outside of diving circles, few people have even heard of the Neptune Islands and Dangerous Reef, where most of the white-shark expeditions are conducted and where almost all of the footage of the great white shark that has ever been used in television documentaries and in Hollywood thrillers was shot.

White-shark expeditions are expensive, typically in excess of U.S.$10,000 by the time you add up airfares and hotels, and they are usually at least 10 days long. For that kind of time and money, it only makes sense to go with the best, and there is little doubt that when it comes to finding great white sharks, the best is Australia's Rodney Fox. After experiencing a serious white-shark attack, Rodney said, "I became such a public person. People were always asking me about the attack, and about great white sharks. I could tell them about the incident, but I soon realized almost nothing was known about the great white. I put together the first-ever filming expedition because I just had to know more." Rodney never really bought in to the myth of the great white as an indiscriminate killing machine, and for the past two decades he has championed the cause of protecting great whites from overzealous fishermen in Australia.

Marine mammals are a favorite food source of great white sharks, and Spencer Gulf has large breeding populations of Australian sea lions and fur seals. Before my last great-white expedition, I decided I wanted to try to film a great white attacking a sea lion. I knew it would make a great sequence for my film *To Be With Sharks*, which premiered in summer 1994 on the Discovery Channel. I wanted to film the action in as realistic a manner as possible, to show nature as it really is.

Great white sharks. Out in the wilderness, just me and my movie camera. Predator and prey. It doesn't get much more macho than this.

One day, a small sea-lion pup showed up around the cage where two great whites were feeding. Instantly, I felt myself trying to holler at the pup to watch out, to get out while the getting was good. But the pup began to chase the sharks and make passes at the bait. Until the pup finally disappeared into the blue, I was terrified for it, knees quivering and beads of sweat dripping down my nose. So much for macho me.

That experience taught me a lot about the way I perceive wildlife and sharks. Sea lions are cute and cuddly. White sharks are anything but. However, those facts alone are no reason to hope that a sea lion survives to prey on fish another day while a white shark goes hungry. The truth is that life in the wild is difficult for both marine mammals and sharks, and each group must make the most of its opportunities.

No doubt about it, after the build-up of tension and a few days of "baiting and waiting," it is a thrill to see a 15-foot (4.5-m)-long shark that weighs in excess of 3,000 pounds (1,350 kg) tear into bait a short distance in front of you. Sheer power, brute force, plain and simple. The predatory capabilities of a great white shark are awesome. I suppose that's what most people go on a white-shark expedition to see. But they come away with much more than thrills. White sharks are stunningly powerful creatures, and it is somewhat eerie how they seem to materialize right in front of you, having come out of nowhere.

Most sharks follow a routine around bait, and their swimming patterns are relatively easy to figure out, but that is not the case with great whites. They swim in a specific pattern just long enough for you to think you have them figured out, and then they come at you from an entirely different direction. It still shakes me up when I am in the cage, staring out into the distance, trying to make out a shape, and I look over my shoulder into the big black eye of a great white.

Of course, it also gives me a chill to watch them materialize and swim right at the cage. In many respects an approaching white shark looks a lot like an underwater missile. Once a great white gets close enough for you to be able to see color and detail, the features I often find myself looking at are the distinctly pointed snout; the enormous girth of the body; the black eye, which tells you nothing about the shark's mood no matter how much you want it to; those rows of triangular, serrated teeth; and the big, powerful tail. Everything about a white shark says "This is my domain."

One of things about white sharks that surprised me, and made a lasting impression, is their distinctive countershading. Light on the underbelly, with darkly colored backs, even large great white sharks often blend in with their surroundings. When they are above you, their whitish underbellies blend with lightly hued surface waters, and when viewed from above, their dark backs blend in with dark reef and kelp on the bottom. It is kind of spooky to watch a 3,000- or 4,000-pound (1,350- or 1,800-kg) shark seem to disappear right in front of your eyes. I have often had a difficult time seeing a white shark I knew was only 30 or 40 feet (9 or 12 m) away, even though visibility was close to 100 feet (30 m).

Of all the photographs I have ever taken, the one image I am most asked about is that of a diver standing on the sea floor, photographing a big great white shark, with no shark cage in sight. The diver is a good friend of mine named Chip Matheson, and the picture was taken in South Australia. We had intentionally decided to get out of the cage with a white shark. That is not something I want to do every day, but I honestly did not think we were taking a risk at the time. I have observed sharks for thousands of hours over the years, and I was confident that the animal was in a mellow mood. In addition, the theory is that adult great whites do not like to feed along the bottom. I was less certain of the validity of that theory than I was of the fact that at that particular moment, that shark was going to be safe and easy to work with.

The shark proved to be rather cooperative, slowly circling us a number of times. Then it would give ground, but soon return and begin to circle again. After the cage had been lowered 50 feet (15 m) to the sea floor, we watched for a while and then exited.

My grandmother, Nana, was a painter, and a painting she did of a camping scene from a trip I took to Montana with my buddy John Hoover is among my favorite possessions. I once asked her how long it took her to create that painting. She told me that she didn't know precisely, but it was several months, and I responded by showing her my photograph of Chip and the great white and gleefully telling her that it took me only $\frac{1}{60}$ of a second to get my shot.

Even though I have been on six expeditions to film the great white, I admit that it's one thing to expect to see a great white in the water as you jump into a shark cage, and quite another to see a great white, or any big shark, when you're outside a shark cage during a normal scuba dive. Even though a big great white is not likely to cause a problem, most of us do have an imagination to deal with.

While it is the size and reputation of a great white shark that make a sighting a thrill, it is the numbers that are overwhelming when you spot a school of scalloped hammerhead sharks. With its bizarre shape, one hammerhead should be enough to raise the hair on your neck; but, with scalloped hammerheads, you can multiply that effect by a 100 or more. Unlike most sharks, which tend to lead solitary lives, scalloped hammerheads gather in schools that consist of several dozen to as many as several hundred individuals. But no matter how much you have heard about what a staggering sight it is to look up and see a big school, there is simply no way to be prepared for the magnitude of impact.

The first time I encountered a school of hammerheads, I was part of an ABC *American Sportsman* film crew shooting an episode about manta rays and hammerheads at the El Baho seamount in the southern end of Mexico's Sea of Cortez. The scene had been described to me before my dive, but nonetheless I was overwhelmed by the sight of 200 or more 7- to 11-foot (2- to 3-m)-long hammerheads appearing out of the blue. There was no sense of panic on the reef.

You might think that fear would be a natural reaction, but few divers who see schools feel fear. I remember feeling a sense of privilege at witnessing such an incredible scene. The sharks just kept coming and coming, from one side of the seamount and then the other. I just held my breath and cowered in the rocks. Soon I had to exhale, and in an instant the sharks began to move away.

As a rule, hammerheads are spooked by the noise created by a diver's exhaust bubbles. That explains the odd-seeming expression voiced by seasoned hammerhead photographers: "Be quiet, or you will scare the sharks!"

Exactly why hammerheads school remains a bit of a mystery. As a general rule, most top-end marine predators lead a more solitary existence. They are unlikely to benefit in any way by collectively warding off potential predators since they are prey to so few, and it takes a lot more small fish or squid to feed hundreds of empty stomachs. Scientists have discovered that the sharks school by day and then hunt alone at night, which eliminates the idea that collective hunting is a motive. Specialists suspect that migration and mating are the keys to the schooling behavior, but no one is absolutely sure.

Typically, when we think of big fish and little fish, we think the latter are probably at risk. But that is not always the case. Scalloped hammerheads, one of eight species of hammerhead, generally inhabit the open ocean, but they visit reef communities to be cleaned by king (genus name *Passer*) angelfish. Sometimes barberfish and juvenile hogfish also provide cleaning services, helping to rid the sharks of ectoparasites.

It is intriguing to watch a hammerhead swim to a cleaning station, turn slightly on its side, and quiver in a display that is a request for cleaning. Soon the small fish will rise high off the reef and begin to peck away at the parasites. Sometimes the hammerheads will line up like cars at a carwash, awaiting their turn.

In the early 1980s I was again searching for hammerheads in the Sea of Cortez, in an area known as Gorda Bank. Often schools of jacks swim over the sharks, and we commonly use them as an aid in locating the schools. By midmorning, we had enjoyed a few brief encounters but nothing out of the ordinary, when I spotted what I thought was a school of jacks below me. At the time, I was free diving (breath-hold diving, using a snorkel but no scuba tank).

Holding my breath, I dived down into the school and suddenly became very disoriented. The bottom of the ocean seemed to be moving. At first I thought we might be having an earthquake. Then I thought something was wrong with the jacks. The school never pulsated; the individual fish never seemed to move. Then it hit me: what I was looking at was not a school of jacks, but instead a group of light markings on the back of a huge whale shark, the world's largest fish.

I surfaced and yelled to my diving buddies. We donned our scuba gear as quickly as we could, and we were soon off for one of my all-time great adventures. Swimming as fast as we could, we caught up with the shark. No doubt about it – this was a big one. The dorsal fin easily rose 4 feet (1.2 m) above the shark's back. The three of us joined up at the pectoral fin on the shark's right side and took a short rest before making a final dash out in front of the face.

The mouth was huge, at least 8 feet (2.4 m) wide, probably wider. The shark had at least a dozen full-grown remoras, also known as hitchhiker fish, on its face, and surprising to me was the fact that a school of several dozen 10- to 20-pound (5- to 9-kg) amberjack were repeatedly swimming inside the shark's mouth, perhaps to feed on parasites. Amberjack are gamefish, but they looked like minnows against the whale shark.

By the time I got out in front of the shark, my legs were beginning to shake from the combination of tiredness and excitement. I was afraid I was at the end of my energy, when suddenly the shark seemed to stop dead in the water. I was able to quit swimming and maintain my position. It was a relief physically, but I feared that I had entered some forbidden zone and that the shark had stopped because it did not approve of my position. About that time my ears started to hurt, and the water began to get cold and dark.

I realized that I was being pushed downward through the water. The shark had not stopped moving, but instead was descending. I had been able to quit kicking because I was being pushed toward the sea floor hundreds of feet below by a wall of water in front of the shark. I didn't feel endangered in any way and was thrilled to have learned about the existence of this wake, something I had never before and have never since heard anyone talk about.

I looked up at my dive buddies, who by then had perched atop the shark's head. Without holding on to or, in fact, touching the shark, they, too, were being pulled along through the water in a slipstream.

I worked my way over to the side of the shark's head, and suddenly found myself hurtling down its body in a current. About midbody, some 20 to 25 feet (6 to 7.5 m) later, I got myself righted and worked my way back to a pectoral fin. My buddies swam to the pectoral fin on the other side of the shark, where they remained for the next 10 minutes or so before we all surfaced. I noticed a look of surprise on their faces during our ascent, and I asked them about it once we got back on the boat.

It turned out that they thought I had run out of air 10 minutes earlier and had already returned to the surface. At that instant, it hit me just how big a whale shark is. Divers on the same shark for 10 minutes could not see one another's bubbles over the whale shark's back. That was a humbling revelation.

Over the past two decades, in places as far apart as Papua New Guinea, the Sudan, and the Bahamas, "shark feeding frenzies" have become a featured attraction of many sport-diving expeditions. The idea is to take part of a day to bait in, or chum, a very hungry, very active group of sharks. The tourists thrill at the sight of the sharks tearing at and competing for the food. The baiting, and sometimes hand feeding, is performed by the divemasters, and the paying customers are positioned in a semicircle around the bait.

Getting within a few feet allows photographers to take action shots of the frenzy, but over the years I have found that the best photo opportunities take place on the periphery of the action, where the sharks have slowed down. The feeding frenzies are not as out of control as they might appear; experienced divemasters can control quite a bit of the action by strategic use of the bait. Given the fact that sharks are so often portrayed as "proverbial eating machines," seeing a feeding frenzy at close range is instructive. There is no question that a diver is outmatched in the shark's natural environment. If a shark wanted to bite a diver, there is not much a diver could do to prevent it. The obvious conclusion is that we are not a preferred part of their natural diet – an important lesson that can be learned from seeing a frenzy "up close and personal."

In addition, it is fascinating to be able to get so physically close to sharks. Despite their reputed ferocity, many sharks are extremely wary around divers, which is a problem from an underwater photographer's point of view. Underwater, if you want crisp, colorful images, you absolutely must be within 8 feet (2 m) of your subject. Closer is always better – in crystal-clear tropical water as well as in more turbid settings.

If a photographer wants to get close to sharks, bait is generally the key. Many of the excellent images of gray reef sharks, silvertips, blue sharks, white sharks, and Caribbean reef sharks have been captured by baiting-in. Whale sharks, basking sharks, and threshers will not be lured in this way, but many types of shark can be enticed to come into photographic range through the use of fish and other food that is part of their natural diet.

The Caribbean and Bahamas are reputed to be great places for divers to see an array of small, colorful reef fish and invertebrates, but many divers seem to think these locations offer no opportunities to see big specimens. My response is that a day of diving at Nassau in the Bahamas with Caribbean reef sharks will change that opinion in a heartbeat. Caribbean reef sharks are big, impressive, and heavy bodied, and swim with an air of confidence and power, never hesitating to pass divers to get to the bait. It usually takes only a few minutes to get the action going, and seeing them is certainly a memorable way to spend a dive or two.

Baiting in sharks also gives divers an opportunity to see details that are likely to be missed during more distant encounters. Almost always, you'll see remoras attached to host sharks, and occasionally see some cleaning behavior, or a small mackerel, pilot fish, or other species "drafting" a shark in much the same manner that bicyclers draft one another.

In many places, if you don't bait, you simply can't get close to sharks, but Costa Rica's Cocos Island is an exception. Located approximately 290 miles (460 km) southwest of the port city of Puntarenas, Cocos is a tiny 15-square-mile (39 km^2) spire surrounded on all sides by deep Pacific waters. It is well known for its enormous populations of scalloped hammerheads and whitetip reef sharks.

While whitetips may not be the scariest-looking of all sharks, they definitely have a sharklike appearance, and with some practice they are often easy to approach, even without the use of bait. By creeping slowly over the bottom, I have often been able to work my way to within 2 feet (60 cm) of whitetips that were resting on the sandy bottom or in caves. The reward for such patience is often a close look at a banded goby providing its cleaning service, or a close-up shot of a mouthful of razor-sharp teeth.

Even after all my years of diving around sharks, I still get excited when I encounter species that I have never seen before or that I want to photograph in a way I never have before. Of course, being in the profession, I want to capture the shark on film, but at this stage of my career, when one more photograph won't make or break me, what I enjoy most is seeing the beauty, power, and grace of a shark in its natural environment, swimming wild and free.

IT IS OFTEN POSSIBLE TO QUICKLY DETERMINE THE SEX OF SHARKS. THE BODIES OF FEMALES, LIKE THAT OF

THE SILKY SHARK PICTURED HERE, ARE OFTEN MARRED BY MATING SCARS.

THE DIVERS ATOP THIS HUGE WHALE SHARK DIDN'T HAVE TO HOLD ON TO GO FOR THEIR UNDERSEA

RIDE. THEY WERE PULLED ALONG BY THE SLIPSTREAM CREATED AS THIS MONSTER MOVED FORWARD.

THE FISH ATTACHED TO THE SHARK'S FACE ARE REMORAS.

LEFT: ONE OF THE ALL-TIME GREAT ADVENTURES FOR SPORT DIVERS IS SPENDING TIME IN A SHARK CAGE IN THE OPEN OCEAN OFF SOUTHERN CALIFORNIA, WHERE BLUE AND MAKO SHARKS ARE OFTEN OBSERVED. SOMETIMES AS MANY AS 50 TO 100 BLUE SHARKS CAN BE ATTRACTED IN A SINGLE AFTERNOON.

❧

BELOW: A BLUE SHARK. ONE OF THE PRIMARY DIFFERENCES BETWEEN WILDLIFE PHOTOGRAPHY ON LAND AND UNDERWATER IS HOW CLOSE THE UNDERWATER PHOTOGRAPHERS MUST GET TO THEIR SUBJECTS IN ORDER TO PRODUCE CLEAR AND COLORFUL IMAGES.

ABOVE: A DIVER INSIDE A CAGE VIDEOTAPES AN
APPROACHING BLUE SHARK IN THE OPEN SEA,
APPROXIMATELY 20 MILES (32 KM) OFF THE
COAST OF SAN DIEGO.

RIGHT: A CARIBBEAN REEF SHARK IS
ATTRACTED TO THE BAIT OFFERED BY A DIVE
LEADER OFF NASSAU IN THE BAHAMAS. THOUGH
NOT EVERYONE'S CUP OF TEA, SHARK DIVING IS
GROWING IN POPULARITY WITHIN THE SPORT-DIV-
ING COMMUNITY.

ABOVE: DIVERS WHO ENCOUNTER SHARKS IN THE WILD ARE

OFTEN STRUCK BY THEIR BEAUTY AS WELL AS THEIR SPEED,

POWER, AND CUNNING.

❧

LEFT: A DIVER DEFTLY LIFTS AN ANGEL SHARK FROM THE SEA

FLOOR. DESPITE THEIR UNTHREATENING APPEARANCE, ANGEL

SHARKS HAVE BIG MOUTHS AND POWERFUL JAWS.

ABOVE: LOCATED ALMOST 300 MILES (480 KM) OUT IN THE PACIFIC, COSTA RICA'S

COCOS ISLAND IS WONDERFUL TO VISIT IF YOU WANT TO PHOTOGRAPH SHARKS AND

RAYS. HERE, A PAIR OF MARBLE STINGRAYS HOVER IN A CURRENT CUT (A GAP IN THE

ROCKS ERODED BY A STRONG CURRENT), WHILE A SCHOOL OF FISH AND A LONE

HAMMERHEAD CRUISE IN THE BACKGROUND.

❧

LEFT: EVEN WHEN GATHERED IN LARGE SCHOOLS, SCALLOPED HAMMERHEADS TEND TO

BE EXTREMELY SKITTISH, AND OFTEN DISAPPEAR WHEN SCUBA DIVERS EXHALE,

RELEASING NOISY BUBBLES. EXACTLY WHY THESE SHARKS SCHOOL REMAINS A MYSTERY

TO SCIENCE, BUT MIGRATION AND MATING MAY BE FACTORS.

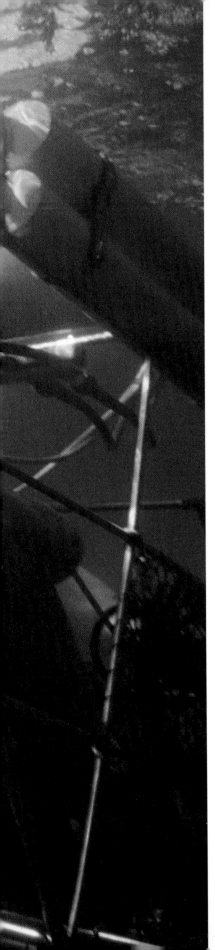

SHARK ATTACKS

WHEN IT COMES TO SHARK ATTACKS, ONE fact stands out prominently. As Richard Ellis so aptly stated in his work *The Book of Sharks*, "Shark attacks are the most publicized and least understood of all aspects of sharks' behavior." Drawing definitive conclusions from the existing data is tricky business. Media reports about shark attacks are often sensationalized and inaccurate. Most of the analyzed scientific data come from areas where English is spoken, which establishes an artificial limit on the data since attacks are not restricted to English-speaking countries. The issue of whether the attack was provoked must also be considered: for example, should an incident in which an underwater cameraman is bitten waving a bleeding fish in a shark's face be classified as a shark attack? Most members of the scientific community would likely say no, but I have read headline-grabbing media reports and watched television news coverage of "shark attack" incidents in which sharks were being baited in.

I do not want to imply that unprovoked attacks do not occur. Clearly, they do. In fact, the day before I wrote this chapter, a commercial diver who was collecting sea

LEFT: A GREAT WHITE SHARK ATTACKS A SMALL MOBILE ANTISHARK CAGE IN THE WATERS OF SOUTHERN AUSTRALIA. APPROXIMATELY HALF OF AUSTRALIA'S COMMERCIAL ABALONE DIVERS USE SOME TYPE OF SURFACE-CONNECTED CAGE TO PROTECT THEMSELVES FROM GREAT WHITE SHARKS.

urchins was fatally attacked at San Miguel Island off the coast of southern California, moments after entering the water. When reading newspapers, listening to radio reports, and watching television news crews comment on this tragic event, I heard various "facts": that this was "the fourth incident of this kind this century," "the eighth incident of this kind since 1921," "the first fatal attack in more than two years," "the first fatality since 1959," and that "approximately 100 shark-attack fatalities occur each year around the world." Inconsistent, or just plain bad, reporting doesn't make the event any less tragic, but it does make it difficult to put the incident into perspective.

Statistically speaking, unprovoked shark attacks on humans are extremely rare. Over a nine-year period, the U.S. Navy documented 1,200 attacks worldwide, 86 percent, or 1,032, of them "unprovoked," but no one really knows how many such incidents occur.

The Shark Attack File, a study headed by Captain David Baldridge of the Mote Marine Laboratory, states that "from 1941 thru 1968, around the world, an average of approximately 26 shark attacks occurred each year." However, in popular books it is quite common to read that approximately 100 shark attacks on humans occur each year. In fact, the Mote study comments on this number, stating "the average number of 26 cases per year is far below the approximately 100 attacks per year often stated in the literature...."

It helps to put shark attacks into perspective when you realize that, worldwide, far more people die from the stings of bees and wasps every year, and in incidents involving elephants, than die from shark attacks.

If shark-attack statistics are going to be used in any kind of meaningful way, the data must be carefully interpreted. For example, it is true that most shark attacks occur during warmer months in relatively shallow water. But what does this finding mean? Does it tell us anything about the feeding patterns of sharks? Or does it simply reflect the fact that a lot more people swim in the ocean during the summer and a lot more of them near shore than out in the middle of the open sea? It is also true that most shark attacks or incidents occur during daylight hours on weekends – a fact that probably relates more to when humans enjoy ocean activities than to the feeding patterns of sharks.

According to the Shark Attack File, in more than three-quarters of cases, shark-attack victims were struck only once and then were let go, not consumed. Perhaps the sharks believed they were biting into something tasty and were fooled, much like thinking you were going to get a bite of steak and ending up with a mouthful of spinach. In response, the sharks left the victims alone. But this conclusion, like many others, is only a matter of speculation. The Mote study also reveals that "91% of the victims were males" but leaves unanswered the question "Why?" Possibly more males than females involve themselves in swimming, snorkeling, surfing, fishing, scuba diving, and other like activities, but not nine times more. Some specialists suspect that it is because males are "more active" in the water, but that, too, is only speculation.

In a very careful analysis of statistics presented in the Mote study, Captain Baldridge was unable to prove any causal relationship between human behavior and unprovoked attacks. Perhaps that is the key to our fascination with shark attacks – their seeming randomness. Maybe if we knew more about exactly what human activity or behavior provoked a shark to attack, we would be more rational about them.

In the popular literature, it is often stated that only 20 or so species are dangerous to humans. A list of the species typically includes the great white, tiger, bronze whaler, bull, blue, great hammerhead, shortfin mako, longfin mako, lemon, dusky, silvertip, gray reef, Caribbean reef, blacktip, Galápagos, silky, oceanic whitetip, reef whitetip, sandbar, tawny nurse, and thresher shark. However, the Shark Attack File study listed "incidents" involving seven-gilled, nurse, wobbegong, ragged tooth, gray nurse, salmon, spinner, dusky, leopard, springer, and a handful of other species as well. I know of several incidents involving Pacific angel sharks and horn sharks that were being handled by divers and snorkelers.

By far the majority of unprovoked attacks on humans take place in tropical and semitropical waters, though attacks are well documented in temperate and polar seas as well. In the United States, the most unprovoked attacks have occurred in southern California, Florida, Texas, and Hawaii. Of course, these states border warm, popular waters and have lots of shoreline. Unprovoked attacks were also documented in Massachusetts and New Jersey.

Worldwide, approximately 35 percent of shark attacks prove fatal. In all cases, the results of the attacks are quite serious, mostly due to enormous loss of blood and body tissue. Interestingly, it is rare for rescuers to be attacked.

Statistically speaking, the most dangerous beach in the world is the resort beach in Amanzimtoti, approximately 17 miles (27 km) south of Durban, South Africa. Between 1940 and 1987, 11 documented attacks occurred there. Three of the attacks were fatal, and six of the attacks took place after antishark nets had been installed. The most likely culprits were great white sharks, but in most cases the sharks were not identified.

Conventional wisdom suggests that swimmers avoid: (1) splashing on the surface; (2) dirty water in which visibility is limited; (3) river mouths or any area where fresh water or garbage is dumped into the sea; (4) seal and sea-lion rookeries, especially during the pupping season; (5) carrying bleeding or struggling fish in the water; (6) any area known to have a lot of sharks; and (7) grabbing, handling, prodding, poking, or riding any shark. I suppose this advice makes at least some sense, though number 7 seems more than obvious, even though the Shark Attack File records a surprising number of incidents provoked by these kinds of activities.

I have often heard divers, even relatively experienced ones, state that a shark approached them aggressively in an attack posture. They generally describe the shark as having "back arched and pectoral fins tucked." This exaggerated body posturing and harried swimming motion is often said to be the typical preattack behavior of many types of shark. However, the only species known to exhibit this agonistic display behavior is the gray reef shark. When posturing, gray reef sharks also tend to swing their heads back and forth while swimming about in a nervous, "herky-jerky" fashion. Though the gray reef's display is not completely understood, researchers believe that it is usually a response to an intruder's getting too close. Sharks are not thought of as being territorial, but, like many other animals, including humans, they do need their own space. Once a gray reef shark begins to display, those who have studied the behavior suggest that the only way to prevent attack is to move quickly away from the shark.

The belief that many sharks exhibit attack postures is probably attributable to the high-profile publicity the gray reef's spectacular display behavior has received on television. It is easy to generalize the behavior of a particular species and mistakenly assume it as common to many species.

Additionally, it is often said that sharks bump their prey before they bite. While that is sometimes the case, it is not always true. In some instances, a shark will initiate contact with a full-on attack, biting on first contact; in other instances, the same shark might circle potential prey repeatedly before bumping or biting. Exactly why a shark might bump its prey before biting is a matter of some debate. It is likely that the shark is testing the potential prey for resistance or trying to determine whether the prey is desirable by using sensory receptors in its skin.

PROTECTION FROM SHARKS

Over the years, a wide variety of shark deterrents, repellents, and other protective devices have been developed. One of the leaders in the effort to create them, the U.S. Navy has spent millions of taxpayers' dollars in efforts to come up with an effective shark deterrent or defense. Early on in the Navy effort, inklike dyes were tested but, despite early optimism, proved to be a dismal failure.

During the Second World War, some pilots were supplied with a portable "shark cage," an inflatable device that was supported by an inner-tube-like float on the surface and which created a solid bag that encompassed the user. The idea was to make the downed pilot "invisible" to the shark, but this device proved to be little more than psychologically comforting to those who didn't know it was essentially useless.

In recent years, some strides have been made with chemical surfactants used to repel sharks. These chemical compounds are highly irritating to the gill tissues of sharks, and they often provoke a fast and very effective flee response. However, there are several problems with the use of surfactants. First, they must be delivered directly into the face or open mouth of an oncoming shark from very close range; second, the delivery must be accurate; and third, if the surfactant is too diluted it loses its effectiveness.

The delivery method also has its problems. Currently, the surfactant is expelled from a gun, using a pressurized CO_2 cartridge or similar device. Reloading is painstakingly slow and must be done on the surface. If the first shot was off target, or more than one shark was involved in a given incident, a single surfactant gun might prove to be of little value. The guns are not huge, but it is difficult to envision a diver equipped with a half-dozen guns attached to his or her body. On the other hand, it is even more difficult for me to envision a need for such measures.

Taser guns that emit electrical shocks underwater have proved effective in recent experiments. However, once again, the user needs to be very close to the shark, and such close quarters allow no room for any problems.

In an effort to protect the safety of the beaches in South Africa and south Australia, a number of communities have utilized large, antishark nets for many years. The heavy mesh nets are strung out in a protective arc around a given beach, and they either ward off the sharks or entangle and drown them. A single net is usually close to 20 feet (6 m) tall and stretches approximately 350 feet (100 m). Tended daily, the nets are typically set in two staggered rows, with the second net serving as a back-up for the first. The nets have helped reduce the number of shark attacks and shark sightings, but even they have not completely eliminated attacks.

A barrier of ascending walls of bubbles created by compressed air released at depth is another technique that has been tried in an effort to keep sharks away from popular beaches. It was hoped that the "wall" or "curtain" of bubbles would repel sharks; however, in tests with tiger sharks, the bubble curtain seemed to have little, if any, effect.

A natural shark repellent is produced by a small fish known as the Moses sole, which is found in the Red Sea. This tiny flatfish secretes a natural repellent that has been shown to stop a shark attack instantaneously, in midbite, much like a surfactant. However, the repellent had to be present in high enough concentrations and accurately delivered. Accumulating adequate concentrations has proved to be impractical, and the problems of delivery are similar to those of surfactants.

Over the years, some divers have used powerheads, sometimes called "bang sticks," as well as CO_2 darts, to repel, wound, or kill sharks. Potent weapons, powerheads are usually some kind of sling-powered underwater explosive that fires on contact with a shark. The diver shoots the powerhead, much like a pole-spear or Hawaiian sling, and the cartridge fires on impact, but powerheads are extremely dangerous and most unforgiving.

CO_2 darts were used prior to the advent of powerheads. The aim was to inject a dart filled with pressurized CO_2 into the body cavity of a shark with a device resembling a pole-spear. Once injected and released, the pressurized gas would expand and cause the shark's body to swell to the point at which the shark became incapacitated. Misfires and bad cartridges led to the darts' being found unsatisfactory as did the fact that penetrating a shark's skin, even with a sharpened dart, is not always easy and, in most cases, requires hitting the shark in the underbelly with the dart.

Sport divers, scientists, and underwater-camera operators have used a variety of antishark cages over the years in order to safely observe sharks from close range. Early cages were made of stainless steel, but today, most people use aluminum and other lighter metals. The cages are typically made of closely spaced bars or wire mesh on all sides, with the exception of a "shooting window" for cameras. Many shark cages are supported by buoyancy control floats, and usually there is some spare air for the divers to use in the event that their supply runs low.

Despite the sound effects dubbed into many television shows, sharks rarely, if ever, attempt to grab a cage and shake it apart. They might bite once or twice, or even shake a little, but as a rule they are quick to let go when they realize that the cage is not food.

The Neptunic antishark suit mentioned earlier, modeled on butchers' gloves and the chain mail worn by knights of old, is a very effective tool for camera operators and scientists who want, or need, to work outside of the safe confines of a shark cage. Though it costs in excess of $8,000 and is tricky to swim in, the suit has proved to be very effective in offering protection against the bites of such species as blue sharks, whitetip reef sharks, wobbegongs, and other small and medium-sized species, but it does not offer sufficient protection against white sharks, tiger sharks, mako sharks, and many other larger sharks.

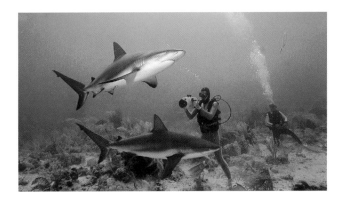

DO THESE DIVERS HAVE ANYTHING TO FEAR? IT'S UNLIKELY. RANDOM ENCOUNTERS WITH SHARKS ALMOST

NEVER PROVE DANGEROUS TO DIVERS UNLESS BAIT IS BEING USED TO ATTRACT THE SHARKS.

ABOVE: THE CARIBBEAN REEF SHARK HAS BEEN DOCUMENTED ATTACKING

HUMANS. IT IS AN IMPRESSIVE, HEAVY-BODIED ANIMAL CAPABLE OF INFLICTING

GREAT DAMAGE WITH A SINGLE BITE.

❧

RIGHT: A 17-FOOT-LONG (5 M) GREAT WHITE SHARK ROCKETS TOWARD ITS

INTENDED PREY ON THE SURFACE. GREAT WHITE SHARKS OFTEN ATTACK ANI-

MALS ON THE SURFACE BY RISING QUICKLY FROM WELL BELOW THEIR VICTIM.

❧

LEFT: ALTHOUGH IT'S NOT ALWAYS THE BEST STRATEGY IN ALL PREDATOR/PREY

RELATIONSHIPS, EXPERIENCED DIVERS OFTEN ADVISE FACING A SHARK AND

LOOKING IT IN THE EYE.

LEFT: JEREMIAH SULLIVAN, CO-DEVELOPER OF THE NEPTUNIC ANTISHARK SUIT, DONS AN EARLY VERSION OF THE PROTECTIVE GARMENT. THE YELLOW PLATES UNDERNEATH ARE MADE OF KEVLAR, THE SAME MATERIAL OFTEN USED IN BULLETPROOF VESTS.

🐋

BELOW: BECAUSE SHARK ATTACKS ARE QUITE RARE, AND BECAUSE THEY REALIZE OUR NATURAL FEAR OF BEING EATEN ALIVE, ATTACKS USUALLY RECEIVE ENORMOUS AMOUNTS OF PUBLICITY.

IN A PERFECT ATTACK, THE TEETH IN THE LOWER JAW OF A GREAT WHITE SHARK MAKE THE FIRST CONTACT WITH THE PREY. THE LONG, NARROW, POINTED TEETH IN

THE LOWER JAW PIN THE PREY, AND THE TEETH IN THE UPPER JAW CUT AND TEAR.

ABOVE: DESPITE THEIR DOCILE APPEARANCE, NURSE SHARKS HAVE BEEN IMPLICATED IN MANY SHARK
ATTACKS. OFTEN THE "ATTACK" WAS PRECIPITATED BY A SWIMMER OR DIVER WHO HAS GRABBED OR
HARASSED THE SHARK IN ONE WAY OR ANOTHER.

Ꙙ

LEFT: AUSTRALIAN SEA LIONS ARE A FAVORITE PREY OF GREAT WHITE SHARKS IN THE WATERS OF SOUTHERN
AUSTRALIA. IT IS OFTEN THEORIZED THAT ATTACKING GREAT WHITES HAVE MISTAKEN SWIMMERS, SURFERS,
AND DIVERS FOR MARINE MAMMALS.

ABOVE: ONE DIVER'S NIGHTMARE IS ANOTHER'S DREAM COME TRUE. HERE A SILKY SHARK CRUISES BELOW THE SWIMSTEP OF A BAHAMIAN DIVE BOAT.

❧

ABOVE (INSET): SHARKS' JAWS ARE PROTRUSIBLE AND ARE NOT FIRMLY ATTACHED TO THE HEAD. WHEN A SHARK OPENS ITS MOUTH TO BITE, THE UPPER JAW EXTENDS FORWARD AND THE TEETH FOLD OUTWARD INTO THE BITING POSITION. AS THE SHARK CLOSES ITS MOUTH, THE TEETH FOLD BACKWARD TOWARD THE STOMACH.

A SCIENTIFIC TEAM LED BY DR. SONNY GRUBER OF THE UNIVERSITY OF MIAMI CONDUCTS A GROWTH-STUDY EXPERIMENT ON A LEMON SHARK IN BIMINI. THE LEMON SHARK IS SAID TO HAVE A "NASTY" TEMPERAMENT, AND ANYONE WORKING WITH IT CLOSE UP NEEDS TO TAKE CARE.

FAR LEFT: AMONG THE MOST DRAMATIC SIGHTS IN ALL OF NATURE IS A GREAT WHITE SHARK WITH ROWS OF RAZOR-SHARP TEETH FULLY EXPOSED!

❧

NEAR LEFT: INHABITING TEMPERATE SEAS AROUND THE WORLD, BLUE SHARKS HAVE BEEN WELL DOCUMENTED ATTACKING HUMANS IN A VARIETY OF CONDITIONS. SURVIVING SHIPWRECK VICTIMS HAVE COMMONLY WITNESSED ATTACKS ON OTHERS CAST ADRIFT.

❧

BELOW: A GREAT WHITE SHARK PROWLS THE REEF. RECENT FINDINGS INDICATE THAT WHITE SHARKS OFTEN CRUISE NEAR THE SEA FLOOR, AND RISE UP SWIFTLY AT PREY ON OR NEAR THE SURFACE.

SHARKS
UNDER SIEGE

THE SHARKS JUST KEPT COMING AND COMING and coming. I honestly don't have any idea how many there were, though I recall estimating 600 when telling some of my closest friends about the experience. I was diving at Darwin Island, the northernmost island in Ecuador's Galápagos archipelago, and I knew it was a great place to dive in hopes of encountering scalloped hammerheads. But my expectations were far exceeded: I had been enveloped in a school of big hammerheads. The biggest problem I had was that every time I tried to film one shark, another got in my way. Some days hammerheads are skittish and wary, but every once in a while they just come and sit in your lap.

After 20 minutes or so, I glanced down at my pressure gauge and realized that despite the spectacular scene in front of me, it was time to make my way back to shallow water. As I was heading back up the reef toward the hang-off line, I noticed a whitish object in the distance. It didn't register until I got closer that I was looking

LEFT: THIS GREAT WHITE SHARK, FILMED IN THE WATERS OF SOUTHERN AUSTRALIA, TRAILS A LINE, LIKELY ACQUIRED DURING AN ENCOUNTER WITH A COMMERCIAL FISHING NET. EVEN LARGE GREAT WHITE SHARKS ARE COMMONLY, THOUGH ACCIDENTALLY, KILLED BY ENTANGLEMENT IN COMMERCIAL FISHING NETS.

at the underbelly of a scalloped hammerhead that was writhing grotesquely on the bottom. The shark was obviously past the point of saving.

The sight made me sick to my stomach. Almost instantly I realized why, as we had pulled up to anchor, another small boat had hurriedly left the site. The small boat was filled with fishermen who were illegally working in protected waters, employing a form of fishing known as "finning," in which only the fins are taken and the rest of the body is dumped back into the sea. Hundreds of sharks are caught and the vast majority of bodies are dumped back into the sea. Wasted.

The writhing hammerhead had been finned alive and then dumped back overboard to suffer until it finally died. My Ecuadorian guide told us the fins were likely headed to the Orient to be used in shark-fin soup.

The scenario reminded me of a similar situation years ago that I had experienced in waters off the coast of southern California. Once again, I had been working with my pal Howard Hall. This time we were shooting film of drift nets that had been set in the middle of the night in an effort to catch swordfish. The aim of the film was to bring public attention to the wastefulness of this type of fishing. Suspended from huge floats out in the open sea, the miles-long nets are made of monofilament mesh, and they extend downward for several hundred feet. Until drift-net fishing was abolished recently by international agreement, the nets set by the international fleet each night were more than enough to circle the world seven times. The nets did catch swordfish and other targeted species, but they also ensnared thousands of blue sharks, sea lions, seals, whales, bat rays, manta rays, and countless other species. The fishermen saw them as nothing more than a nuisance. As soon as they could remove them from the nets, they were going to dump their bodies back into the sea. Not one ounce of meat or skin would ever be used for anything, except perhaps occasionally as bait for other fisheries. Killed, cursed, and thrown overboard was the fate suffered by most of these creatures, referred to as "incidental kill," a way of distinguishing them from the targeted species.

I will never forget the gut-wrenching experience of diving the nets at four o'clock in the morning and seeing blue sharks and sea lions hanging lifelessly. It was not just the fact that they had been killed that was so disturbing, but that the killing had been "incidental," needless.

A study conducted on the Japanese gill-net fleet in 1990 showed that as many as 41 million unwanted individuals were tragically killed in the gill nets of their fleet alone. Of these, approximately 700,000 were sharks.

While the United Nations did, in 1992, announce a worldwide ban on gill netting, compliance is another matter. The fleets of many key nations, especially those in Asia, have been known to violate the ban on a regular basis. Unfortunately, fishermen from many nations still fin sharks. All over the world, not only are sharks being exploited, but shark species are being decimated as humans overfish entire populations.

Trawlers and longliners continue to make their presence felt. Many swordfishermen prefer to longline, but their hooks catch sharks as well as swordfish. Once again, the sharks are often viewed only as a nuisance, and their bodies are dumped into the sea to rot. Industry experts state that for every swordfish caught, two sharks are killed and wasted.

The U.S. National Marine Fisheries Service maintains that the shrimp-trawling industry in the Gulf of Mexico wastes more than 2,800 tons of sharpnose sharks each year. It's the irresponsible misuse and mismanagement, the wastefulness, the short-sighted disrespect for the natural world that I find most appalling.

If anywhere in the world people were doing to whales, dolphins, seals, sea lions, or any other marine mammal the things they are doing to individual sharks and to shark populations, the public outcry would be overwhelming. Unfortunately, sharks are not cute and cuddly, furry creatures with big, sad eyes that automatically garner public sympathy.

As simplistic as this concept may seem, it really is at the core of the issue. As the guardians of this planet, our species simply does not value sharks as much as we value many other animals. Ask almost anyone to name the most dangerous animals on earth, and the odds are that the list won't go on very long before you hear the word "shark." You will probably have time for lunch and a nap before our own species makes the list. This prevailing attitude contributes greatly to the fact that people in many nations turn a blind eye to the horribly wasteful overexploitation of sharks.

The facts demonstrate that people kill a lot more sharks every year than sharks kill people. While not all shark attacks on humans are reported, it is generally agreed that, worldwide, sharks kill fewer than 100 people per year.

By comparison, people annually kill more than 100 million sharks. Some scientists fear that as many as five shark fisheries will be rendered no longer commercially viable by the year 2025. Many experts believe this estimate to be grossly overoptimistic. In some instances, shark populations have not rebounded from overfishing even as long as 50 years after the commercial fishery collapsed. Currently, many scientists warn of the threat of heavy-fishing pressure to populations of shortfin mako sharks off the coast of California and Baja California, lemon sharks in Bimini, scalloped hammerheads from Baja California to the Galápagos Islands, and many more. Australian fisheries have severely depleted gummy-shark populations, and in recent years, in the waters off Europe, commercial fishermen from Ireland take as many as 1,000 basking sharks every year for engine oil derived from their livers. This number is thought to be far more basking sharks than the population can produce.

SHARK CONSERVATION

I suppose an obvious question to address is "Why should we care about sharks?" Should we should put economic pressures and restriction on other nations if they abuse shark populations, and should we put stronger, more environmentally minded legislation in place to regulate shark fisheries within our own boundaries? Many people believe it morally wrong to eliminate any species from the face of the earth if its eradication can be prevented. Beyond the moral and ethical considerations, scientists are quick to point out that sharks play a variety of vital roles in many ocean ecosystems.

Great whites, blues, makos, bulls, silkies, scalloped hammerheads, tigers, silvertips, lemon sharks, and other species fill the niche of apex, or top-end, predator in their respective food chains. Apex predators help to cull out weakened, sick, and old members of prey populations, which range from bottom-dwelling echinoderms, crustaceans, and mollusks, to fish, turtles, sea lions, seals, dolphins, and whales. The bottom line is that sharks help to keep prey populations strong by eliminating the weak from the gene pool.

Sharks also help maintain a balance by preventing prey populations from expanding to unhealthy levels. The balance of nature can be dramatically upset if the populations of individual species greatly expand or diminish. Though it often takes longer to see an impact when top-end predators are removed from a food chain than it does when plants and animals at the lower end are removed, ultimately the results are equally devastating.

Many shark fisheries have expanded greatly in the past decade or two. Statistics indicate that, worldwide, the total take of commercial shark fisheries increased by more than 30 times during the 1980s alone. The vast majority of the catch is consumed by humans, though sharks also have other uses, including pet food. For many years, sharks were marketed as grayfish, flake, or steakfish simply because many grocers and restaurateurs found that people wouldn't order shark. Today, however, species such as shortfin mako sharks, thresher sharks, porbeagles, catsharks, and even spiny dogfish are considered to be culinary treats in many places.

In Britain, as many as 12,000 metric tonnes of spiny dogfish sharks are consumed on an annual basis by the fish-and-chips industry alone. In the United States, the total shark take from commercial fisheries increased tenfold, from 1,200 tons in 1986 to more than 12,000 tons in 1989. In 1993, it is estimated that a total of 488,000 coastal sharks were caught by commercial fishermen in the United States.

The serious cause for concern is not the large increase in the takes but the fact that studies conducted by scientists from the National Marine Fisheries Service report that the combined recreational and commercial shark take exceeds the maximum sustainable yield of the combined populations by more than 5,900 tons. In other words, 5,900 more tons of sharks are being removed than shark populations can reproduce in U.S. waters alone. It doesn't exactly take a math major to interpret the handwriting on the wall.

In other parts of the world, the pressure on shark populations is even greater. In Hong Kong alone, more than 7 million pounds (3 million kg) of shark fins are imported every year to make shark-fin soup. Considered to be an aphrodisiac as well as highly sought after culinary fare, shark fins command high prices in many Asian nations. Blue sharks and hammerheads are usually the most desired species, but the fin fisheries are expanding. Increased demand has led to dramatic price increases. The price of shark fins rose by as much as 130 percent in the U.S. market in the last half of the 1980s, while the total shark catch off Florida increased by 500 percent during that same time frame.

During an 11-year period, extreme pressure on the spiny-dogfish population in British Columbia reduced the total take by 75 percent. Similarly, in the 1930s, pressure on soupfin sharks all but eliminated the species from the San Francisco Bay, and in only a few years an angel-shark fishery in southern California has dramatically reduced the population.

When I first started diving in southern California almost 20 years ago, angel-shark sightings were common in many places. After less than a decade of exploitation by the angel-shark fishery, it is difficult to know where to go to see an angel shark. In fact, this past fall I had hoped to film angel sharks at Catalina Island with the help of students in a doctoral program, studying with Dr. Donald Nelson at Cal State Long Beach. The problem was that these specialists couldn't find enough sharks to warrant an expedition.

Equally as threatening is the fact that a few years ago the California Department of Fish and Game discovered that mako sharks, whose populations were dramatically reduced, used inshore waters as a nursery area. Officials wanted to place a moratorium on fishing for makos inshore. The fishermen responded to the moratorium by saying that they were not able to endure the expense of fishing more distant waters, and they turned their efforts toward fishing blue sharks.

Unfortunately, blue-shark meat spoils very quickly, within minutes, if the shark is not skinned immediately after death; uric acid spills into the meat and renders it useless for human consumption. The fishermen boldly stated that they didn't care if the market was pet food, they could not afford any alternatives.

Frankly, I sympathize with the plight of the fishermen. One reason is that I like them. In many ways, commercial fishermen seem like the last of the pioneers. They have hard lives, and few, if any, are doing better than just getting by. But no matter how much I admire them, I know we cannot allow wasteful fisheries to continue.

Shark skin used in purses, wallets, belts, watch straps, and boots is also in high demand. Markets in Japan import more than U.S.$1.2 million worth of shark skin every year to make purses. Shark-skin products are also very popular in the United States, where the handbag market alone imports almost $1 million worth of sharks. Throughout Europe, shark-skin watchbands are becoming increasingly popular, and shark jaws and teeth are sold in curio shops around the world.

Recreational fishing is also a contributing factor. As recently as the 1940s and 1950s, most sport-fishing enthusiasts didn't really view sharks as highly prized gamefish. But things have changed dramatically in the past five or six decades, especially in the United States, as the populations of many species of gamefish such as albacore, swordfish, and dorado have declined. The shark take has markedly increased, and shark-fishing tournaments, where prize money is often more than $25,000, are gaining in popularity.

In the western Atlantic, the number of sharks taken by sportfishermen increased more than sixfold between 1965, when 2,600 tons were caught, and 1980, when almost 16,000 tons of sharks were taken. But that number has declined steadily since 1982. In 1989, less than 400 tons of shark were taken by East Coast sport fishermen. No moratoriums have been enforced; efforts to catch sharks have not decreased.

Sadly, many specialists maintain that there are simply fewer sharks to catch.

As a result of these and other case histories, many specialists warn that intensive, unregulated fishing pressure on shark populations will result in the collapse of fisheries and, worse yet, could result in biological extinction. Doubters are often unaware that all too often, overpressured wildlife populations "crash" suddenly rather than undergoing a gradual decline.

Shark Biology and Preservation

Animals have a wide variety of reproduction strategies. Some produce numerous offspring but offer very little parental care. This strategy leads to survival based on sheer numbers. Other creatures expend significant amounts of energy in providing extremely attentive parental care, but these animals usually produce a comparatively small number of offspring.

Some creatures grow rapidly, mature relatively early, and have high reproductive rates. The life strategy of the shark is characterized by slow growth, late maturation, and low reproductive rates.

Whereas many bony fish reproduce within less than a year after their own birth, many sharks are thought to reach sexual maturity after 10 years, and some species probably after 15 years or more. Further compounding the issue is the fact that the gestation period for some sharks is as long as 24 months. After all that, the litter sizes are often smaller than one dozen young, while lemon sharks, like white sharks, produce only two young, one in each uterine canal.

As long as living conditions are relatively stable, creatures like sharks tend to flourish. But entire populations are especially susceptible to sudden environmental changes and catastrophic natural events. In bony fish, a relatively small number of fertile females are capable of rebuilding a population in a fairly short time, but that is far from the case with sharks. In many species of shark, a single sexually mature individual represents a significant amount of the reproductive energy of the entire population.

SAVING SHARKS

If we look at the value of sharks in economic terms, a good argument can be made in many parts of the world that a live shark is worth far more than a dead one. In southern California, New Jersey, Australia, the Bahamas, the Sudan, Micronesia, Papua New Guinea, and many other locations, sport divers spend big bucks to dive with sharks. I know of one small operator in the Bahamas who generated more than $400,000 in a single year from shark dives alone. This money is "earned" by a population of approximately 50 to 100 animals.

Compare that income with the 50 cents per pound a fishermen might make for 75 sharks weighing 150 pounds (68 kg). The numbers don't even come close. And tourist dollars spent in shops, restaurants, hotels, and airlines are extra. If protected and promoted, sharks can be a big business in the ecotourism trade in some places.

If sharks are going to be able to survive the fishing onslaught, several things need to be done. First, a significant amount of research needs to be conducted. It is an economic reality that most fisheries-biology studies are done on economically viable species that have produced for years. It seems to take scientists and fisheries authorities a while to gear up for a study. As long as the catch size is increasing, there often seems little need for extensive research. In too many instances, the scientists are not called in until the total take declines.

Shark fisheries often develop and collapse within a very short time frame. Little is known about the natural histories and population dynamics of many species, and by the time a study is conducted, the baseline data are already skewed. However, some studies and fieldwork are far better than none at all. Scientists can still contribute valuable information to the effort to save many shark populations by learning about such factors as population sizes, home ranges of various species, litter sizes, the locations of nursery areas, life expectancy, and growth rate. This knowledge can help fisheries personnel implement policies and regulations so that shark populations can be managed in a responsible manner.

In order for a protection effort to be successful, money and public support are required. Most, but not all, of the funding will likely originate from taxes levied against commercial and sport fishermen. But, eventually, significant support from the general public will be necessary. Public education regarding the decline of shark populations as a result of overfishing could certainly help, and a public-relations campaign to combat the myth that surrounds sharks would likely help as well. Australia was the first modern nation to protect any species of sharks, but in the past few years a number of countries have followed suit. A lot of effort was required to move the bureaucracies in charge, but it did get done. As more and more people learn about sharks, and as more people become aware of the problems they face, I see more reason to hope that the public's mood will shift, and the "save the sharks" movement will gain support.

Vic Hislop with giant artificial jaws outside his Sharkshow at Cairns.

GREAT WHITE
HUNTER

Summer means shark alerts, and controversial hunter Vic Hislop wants known man-eaters destroyed. But the Fisheries Department says he is irrational and anti-conservationist.

ROBERT REID speaks to the killers' killer in Cairns.

ABOVE: THIS BLUE SHARK APPEARS TO BE THE LUCKY SURVIVOR OF AN ENCOUNTER WITH A GILL NET OR A FISHHOOK. ALL OVER THE WORLD, SHARK POPULATIONS ARE BEING DRASTICALLY REDUCED BY COMMERCIAL FISHING. IN ALL TOO MANY CASES THE SHARKS ARE VIEWED BY THE FISHERMEN AS INCIDENTAL KILL, AND THEIR RAVAGED BODIES ARE DUMPED BACK INTO THE SEA TO ROT.

❧

LEFT: UNFORTUNATELY, OVER THE YEARS, IN MANY SOCIETIES, CATCHING AND KILLING SHARKS HAS BEEN VIEWED AS AN ACT OF COURAGE AND PROOF OF MANHOOD.

BELOW: NETS THAT ARE LOST AT SEA (GHOST NETS) CONTINUE TO KILL HUGE NUMBERS OF SHARKS AND MANY OTHER MARINE ANIMALS FOR MANY YEARS.

BELOW (INSET): SHARK FINS DRYING BEFORE BEING SHIPPED TO THE FAR EAST, WHERE SHARK FIN SOUP IS CONSIDERED A DELICACY. ALL TOO OFTEN, SHARK-FINNING FISHERIES HAVE PROVED TO BE EXTREMELY WASTEFUL, AS THE REST OF THE SHARKS' BODIES GO UNUSED.

ABOVE (TOP): ONCE QUITE COMMON IN THE WATERS OF SOUTHERN CALIFORNIA, SWELL SHARK SIGHTINGS HAVE BECOME RATHER RARE IN RECENT YEARS.

❧

ABOVE (BOTTOM): MAKO SHARKS, LIKE SO MANY SPECIES AROUND THE WORLD, HAVE BEEN SEVERELY OVERFISHED IN MANY AREAS. FISHERY STATISTICS INDICATE THAT THEIR NUMBERS HAVE DECREASED DRAMATICALLY.

❧

LEFT: QUITE COMMON IN THE NEAR SHORE WATERS OF SOUTHERN CALIFORNIA AS RECENTLY AS A DECADE AGO, PACIFIC ANGEL SHARK POPULATIONS ARE THOUGHT TO BE DIMINISHING. THESE LIE-IN-WAIT PREDATORS TEND TO HAVE A VERY SMALL HOME RANGE, AND AS A RESULT LOCAL POPULATIONS CAN BE QUICKLY DEPLETED BY COMMERCIAL FISHING.

SELECTED BIBLIOGRAPHY

Cleave, Andrew. *Sharks: A Portrait of the Animal World.* Leicester, England: Magna Books, 1994.

Douglass, Stacy, and Darren Douglass. "Sand Tigers." *Diver* 15/5 (January-February 1990).

Ellis, Richard. *The Book of Sharks.* New York: Alfred A. Knopf, Inc., 1983.

Harding, John H. "Return of the Gray Nurse Shark." *Sea Frontiers*, July-August 1990.

Howorth, Peter C. *Sharks: The Story Behind the Scenery.* Las Vegas, NV: KC Publications, 1991.

Mannucci, Maria Pia, and Alessandro Minelli. *The Great Book of the Animal Kingdom.* Rome, Italy: Arch Cape Press, 1982.

McRae, Michael. "Misunderstood Predator." *Equinox*, October 1992.

Raven, Peter H., and George B. Johnson. *Biology.* St. Louis, MO: Mosby, 1986.

Server, Lee. *Sharks.* New York: Crescent Books, 1989.

_____. *The World of Nature: Sharks.* New York: Gallery Books, 1990.

Snyderman, Marty. "Diving the Outer Edge of Adventure." *Skin Diver*, April 1980.

_____. "California Sea Lions: Cavorting Clowns of the Pacific Kelp." *Skin Diver*, September 1980.

_____. "Sitting on a Seamount." *Oceans* 5 (September 1981).

_____. "Sharks of the Open Sea." *Diver* 9/4 (June 1983).

_____. "A Point Defense Against Sharks." *Proceedings*, August 1985.

_____. *California Marine Life.* Port Hueneme, CA: Marcor, 1987.

_____. "How to Photograph Sharks." *Ocean Realm*, Winter 1988.

_____. *The Living Ocean.* New York: Image Bank, 1989.

_____. *Ocean Life.* Lincolnwood, IL: Publications International, 1991.

_____. "On Photographing Sharks." *Sea Frontiers* 38/6 (November-December 1992).

_____. "Shark Expeditions: Where Divers Go to Swim with Sharks." *Scuba Times* 15/2 (March-April 1994).

Snyderman, Marty, and M. Tundi Agardy. *Life in the Sea.* Lincolnwood, IL: Publications International, 1994.

Snyderman, Marty, and Clay Wiseman. *Guide to Marine Life of the Caribbean, Florida and Bahamas.* Locust Valley, NY: Aqua Quest, 1995.

Steel, Rodney. *Sharks of the World.* New York: Facts On File, 1985.

Stevens, John D., et al. *Sharks.* Hong Kong: Intercontinental, 1987.

Sumich, James L. *Biology of Marine Life.* Dubuque, IA: Wm. C. Brown, 1976.

Sutton, Laurie, and Marty Snyderman. *Sharks.* Grand Cayman: Sea D Rom, 1994.

Taylor, Geoff. "Big Fish Story." *BBC Wildlife* 11/8 (August 1993).

INDEX